"Surely a beach house would be too intimate for work late at night."

Noah Seaton chuckled. "Not at all."

Candle O'Shea wasn't used to being dismissed so lightly. Not that she intended for a moment to chase after this man as others had apparently done, but neither did she like being treated like a wall fixture!

Mr. Seaton's explanation, however, took another turn. "I would require you to stay at the house until my thesis is finished, Miss O'Shea. But the place isn't small, and under the eye of my housekeeper, the arrangement will be far from intimate."

"I see," Candle said, glad for the sunburn that hid her embarrassment.

"Will you come with me, then?" he asked with a strange mixture of business-like urgency and little-boy appeal. "I give you my word that you'll be provided for and that I'll not be overbearing."

Candle smiled at his rather impish grin. "And, I'm to take you at your word?"

The grin vanished, and Mr. Seaton became serious again. "In my business, Miss O'Shea, my word is usually enough."

"And, what," she finally thought to ask, "*is* your business?"

Seaton glanced at the highly amused Mrs. Powers, then turned back to Candle.

"I assumed you knew, but of course you couldn't. I'm a clergyman, Miss O'Shea."

Candle

MARY HARWELL SAYLER

BOOKS
of the Zondervan Publishing House
Grand Rapids, Michigan

A Note from the Author:

I love to hear from my readers! You may write to:
      Mary Harwell Sayler
      Author Relations
      1415 Lake Drive, S.E.
      Grand Rapids, MI 49506
      Please enclose a self-addressed, stamped envelope
      if you'd like a personal response.

CANDLE
Copyright © 1988 by Mary Harwell Sayler

Serenade/Serenata is an imprint of Zondervan Publishing House,
1415 Lake Drive, S.E., Grand Rapids, MI 49506.

ISBN 0-310-47531-7

Scripture quotations are taken from the *Holy Bible: New International Version* (North American Edition), copyright © 1973, 1978, 1984, by the International Bible Society, used by permission of Zondervan Bible Publishers.

Edited by Sandra L. Vander Zicht
Designed by Kim Koning

Printed in the United States of America

88 89 90 91 92 / DP / 10 9 8 7 6 5 4 3 2 1

To my beloved friend,
Sue Wiatt
of There Is More Ministries,
Balsam Grove, North Carolina,
with love and thanks
for your strong faith in God,
your sound teaching in his church,
your powerful, perceptive prayers,
and your belief
in me.

4493

How lovely are Your tabernacles, O Lord of hosts! My soul yearns, yes, even pines and is homesick for the courts of the Lord.
(Psalm 84:1–2, *The Amplified Bible*)

chapter
1

THE FLORIDA SUN RAKED CANDLE'S FAIR SKIN, and she woke
with a start. How could she have been so careless as to fall
asleep? This wasn't the bone-chilling winter climate to which
she was accustomed! Only last night, her dinner companion
had warned her to use sunscreen and good sense whenever
she went out. Unfortunately, she'd done neither.

"Don't take a chance," Brad had cautioned over their
seafood-heaped platters. "With your milky skin and red hair,
you'd be miserable in no time."

This morning, however, Brad's advice had seemed incon-
gruous with the soft early rays of a January sky. A light breeze
masked the seventy-eight-degree temperature. Candle hadn't
bothered to look at the thermometer outside the beach
cottage window.

She had dressed appropriately, she'd thought, wearing a
two-piece terry beach suit that protected her arms and legs.
But the outfit exposed a generous section of midriff, and,
when she'd settled comfortably on the padded chaise near the
shore, she'd soon pushed up the elastic cuffs on her sleeves
and pants. How good it felt to relax, to be enveloped by
gentle warmth!

She was tired, not from the date with Brad, but from the

insomnia that comes with indecision and adjustments. The sun's reflection on the water had hurt her pale green eyes, and rather than go back for her sunglasses, she'd closed her lids against the glare—a mistake, she now realized! The rhythmic shh-sha-shh of the sea waves had soothed her, and she'd quickly fallen asleep.

Looking now at her wristwatch, Candle judged the nap to have lasted a couple hours. Maybe more. But, even on its noon approach, the placid sky seemed harmless enough. Surely this mild exposure couldn't result in a bad burn. Or could it? With alarm, she noticed that her arms and legs had begun to splotch.

"Just what I need!" Candle scolded herself.

She would look awful for this afternoon's interview. But she couldn't cancel. She needed a job, any job that Temporary Services would offer. Even a short-term position could mean the difference between staying in this restful paradise or returning home prematurely to snow and ice—and Gary.

If Candle went back now, she knew that Gary Woodward's attentions would be stifling. He had promised to give her time to think over his unexpected marriage proposal, and time was what Candle intended to take. She liked Gary—and was attracted to him—but some flaw in their relationship disturbed her; she couldn't quite put her finger on it. Away from him, she could at least think clearly.

Scooping up her unused towel, Candle headed for the beach cottage that belonged to her friend Marcy John. Her long legs carried her in slow motion across the deep, dry sand of low tide, and with each step, Candle became more painfully aware of exposed skin. Pausing, she caught her breath, and glancing toward the cottage, she spotted Marcy waving gaily from the cypress deck. Candle quickened her pace.

"Ready for lunch?" Marcy called out. "I brought home tons

of paper, so I won't have to go back to the office after—Good grief! You look dreadful!"

Candle managed a grim smile. "I hope it's not that bad."

"H'm. See for yourself. What on earth happened?"

"I fell asleep for a couple of hours."

Marcy shook a dark mop of curls in disbelief. "You didn't! That sounds like something *I'd* do, not you."

"If you had, you'd only get browner," Candle said. "I don't suppose you've ever had a burn occur as fast as this one?"

Marcy shook her head again. "But I don't know if you have a burn."

"What else could it be?"

"An allergic reaction."

"Marcy! If that was meant to comfort, it didn't! My appointment is in two hours!" Candle glanced at her watch. "No! Less than that. What am I going to do? I can't cancel now."

"I know! I know! But while we're standing here talking, you're puffing up like a soufflé. A cold shower might help. Stay in as long as you can stand it," Marcy ordered, and Candle hurried to comply.

The cool water needled Candle's tender skin, and all of the warmth she'd felt earlier evaporated. When she'd turned off the tap, she toweled herself gingerly and surveyed the damage in the bathroom mirror. It was even worse than she'd thought!

Her nose, usually slender, had broadened across the bridge, and her full lips were fuller. Her wide-set almond-shaped eyes seemed closer together, and somehow they'd shrunk beneath swollen lids and cheeks. She looked a decade older than her twenty-five years.

If her one-thirty appointment hadn't been so crucial,

Candle might have found her sudden loss of beauty amusing. Now she simply wondered what to do. She couldn't call the agency from the cottage since it had no phone, and Marcy, if she'd heard right, wasn't planning on returning to her office that afternoon.

The only solution, Candle decided, was to present her predicament to the agency and go ahead with the necessary tests and application forms. She'd probably have to wait a few days before Temporary Services would have a position for her anyway. And she hoped by then she'd be back to normal.

With a lightened heart, Candle dressed with care. She chose a loose-fitting smock with flowing sleeves and tossed aside the belt. It did nothing for her figure, but neither did it chafe her flaming skin. Brushing her dark red hair away from her swollen face, she twisted the thick mane into a tight bun and pinned it against the nape of her neck. There. That would have to do. A piece of jewelry or a touch of makeup might have improved her looks, but the thought of either made her want to scream.

"What do you think?" she asked Marcy, who was busily tossing a salad of celery and shrimp.

"Awful." Marcy clapped her hand across her mouth. "Sorry. But if I didn't know who you were, I'd never recognize you."

"Oh, dear."

"It's not one of your glowing moments," Marcy quipped, "but it won't last. Come on. Lunch is ready. Maybe some food will make you feel better."

Candle doubted it, but she appreciated her friend's concern. More than once Marcy's generosity and good humor had helped her through confusing times with Gary; even now, she was here at Marcy's insistence. When she'd written to share her ambivalent feelings about Gary's proposal, Marcy had suggested she hold off making any decisions and come to Florida. So she had. But since then, they had not broached the subject.

"Do you dislike Gary?" Candle asked now as she bit into the curls of pink-veined shrimp.

Marcy glanced up with questioning brows. "Dislike him? Not really. Why?"

Candle smiled. "Just wondering."

Her friend stalled, offering more herb tea. "Gary seems nice enough," she said hesitantly, "but . . ."

"But what? Tell me, Marcy. I want to know."

Marcy drew a deep breath and blurted out, "He's not right for you."

Candle speared a chunk of celery. "How can *you* be so sure when I'm not?"

Marcy sipped her honey-sweetened tea. "You're open, honest, trusting. . . . With Gary I have the feeling there's someone else under the surface."

Candle frowned, wondering if Marcy was expressing what she herself felt. For more than two years she'd worked with Gary and always found him amiable. Yet, he always got what he wanted. Sometimes she wondered what would happen if he didn't.

"Hey!" her friend said now, ending the conversation. "Advice is cheap, but shrimp isn't! Hurry with your salad, or you'll be late."

Candle laughed. "The salad is excellent, and we'll see about the advice." She rinsed the bowl when she'd finished, grabbed her car keys, and headed toward the door. "I wish you'd been home last night when Brad picked me up. I wondered what you'd think of him." She had a feeling that Marcy would like him a lot.

With Brad on her mind, Candle slid into her two-seater

sports coupe and turned on the powerful engine. She'd met Brad only recently. He seemed nice enough, but she couldn't see herself becoming terribly interested. Too bad. He was certainly thoughtful—a trait she admired in men. When he'd discovered she loved classical music, he'd promised to wrangle last-minute tickets for a Bach concert tonight.

"But you said you don't like Bach," she'd protested.

"I never met the guy."

Candle had laughed. "Well, the concert sounds delightful," she'd assured him. But now it didn't.

The thought of heels and hose and crisp fabric, scratching, made her groan, but it seemed a shame for those tickets to go to waste. Maybe Marcy would enjoy an evening out. Maybe Marcy would enjoy Brad! They really would make a lovely couple—so well suited, she thought. With the matchmaking settled in her own mind, Candle resolved to phone Brad from the employment agency. If he didn't object, she could ask Marcy as soon as she got home.

Sunlight poured into the small car, warming its interior. Candle squirmed uncomfortably. When she'd switched off the ignition, she peered at her image in the rear-view mirror and immediately wished she hadn't. Bumpy clusters shone under tightened skin. The effect was appalling! *Lord, you promised to make all things work to the good of those who love you,* Candle reminded him in prayer, *but I'm not sure how you'll do it: I'm a mess!*

Getting out of the car, she quickly crossed the hot pavement and stepped into the mercifully cool office of Temporary Services. It was smaller than she'd expected. An empty desk stood in the back of the room and another toward the front door. From a squeaking chair, a woman stared at her.

"Excuse me," Candle said. "I have an appointment with a Mrs. Powers."

CANDLE

Pretending to concentrate on the folder in front of her, the woman had lowered her eyes, but now they flew open. "I'm Mrs. Powers. But you're not . . ." She glanced again at the folder marked "O'Shea."

"I'm Candle Louise O'Shea."

"But . . . but we asked for a recent photo, and, uh . . ."

"I know. It doesn't look like me. That's what I've come to explain."

Her reasons evoked such empathy that Mrs. Powers visibly softened. "You really should see a doctor, dear. But, by all means, let's go ahead with the paperwork today. We can get your typing and shorthand tests out of the way, if you like."

Candle agreed readily. Despite swollen fingers, she completed the tests speedily. Then, while Mrs. Powers tallied the results, she penciled in a batch of forms. Her head throbbed slightly, and she was glad when Mrs. Powers, having finished the tally, motioned her back to the chair beside her desk.

"You've done remarkably well, Miss O'Shea. In fact, I can't recall when anyone has had a better score."

"I hope that means I won't be difficult to place."

"I should think not. Of course," Mrs. Powers added as she scanned Candle's file, "your temporary employer might not be able to match the nice salary you earned at Woodward Publishing."

"I expected that. But I hope it won't be too great a cut."

"I'll do my best." Mrs. Powers glanced at the application form. "It says here you left Woodward Publishing for personal reasons."

"Actually, I've only taken a leave of absence."

"For how long?"

"I'm not sure."

"I see," Mrs. Powers said, although she clearly didn't. She looked as though she'd love to ask what the personal reasons

15

were, but assumed, correctly, that Candle had no intention of telling her.

Instead, Mrs. Powers asked, "What brings you to Florida?"

"A friend of mine—Marcy John," Candle answered. "She's in advertising—has her own small business. We've known each other for ages, but she moved to Florida a number of months ago, bought a beach cottage, and raved about it until I had to come down." That this was only partial information was really none of Mrs. Powers's business.

"How nice." Mrs. Powers leafed through the application forms absently until her eyes caught a blank. "Oh, dear. You don't have a phone number? That could be a problem, Miss O'Shea. You see, I have a reputation of providing the best service in the shortest amount of—"

Before Mrs. Powers could finish, and before Candle could assure her that she would call the agency once a day, twice if necessary, the door flew open, and a tall figure stormed into the office. The man's agitation piqued Candle's curiosity, and to her chagrin, she found herself staring at the handsome but angry face much as Mrs. Powers had previously gaped at her. He was in his mid-thirties, Candle judged, and obviously used to having his own way.

"For the fourth time this month, Mrs. Powers, you've sent me another beauty with a rag-mop brain," the deep voice thundered. "How can I make it clearer? That will not do!"

Looking mortified, Mrs. Powers managed to ask the man his name.

"Noah Seaton!" he barked, then added caustically, "I wasn't aware that you had so many clients you couldn't remember their names."

Somehow Mrs. Powers regained enough composure to remark coldly, "I can assure you, Mr. Seaton, I will not forget you in the future."

A chuckle escaped Candle's swollen lips, and the sound caught Noah Seaton's attention. His dark eyes took in the tight chignon, and the loose dress. If Candle thought he'd dismiss her, she was entirely wrong.

"Now *that*," he said, with a sweep of an arm, "is the type of woman I've been begging your agency to send! Someone mature and no-nonsense. But, instead you keep wasting my time with young lovelies who answer to Tanya or Anastasia or . . ." He turned to Candle and demanded, "What *is* your name, by the way?"

Obediently, she answered, "Louise O'Shea," surprising both herself and Mrs. Powers by excluding her first name.

"See!" Mr. Seaton exclaimed triumphantly. "Louise! A sensible name for a sensible woman. And she's efficient too, isn't she?" he queried, already certain of the answer.

"Yes, quite efficient." Over her initial shock, Mrs. Powers appeared to be enjoying herself. "Miss O'Shea has completed her skills tests if you'd care to look over the results. She has, in fact, one of the top scores of any of our applicants."

"That doesn't say much," Seaton remarked beneath his breath. Aloud he said, "She'll do fine, I'm sure."

"Splendid!" Mrs. Powers exclaimed with the relief of one who had just solved two difficult problems in a single gesture.

"If you'll send her to my beach house immediately, we can get started this afternoon."

He'd turned his back and started for the door when Candle bolted from her chair. "Wait just one minute!" Her face blazed red, more from anger than from sun. "I'm not at all sure I intend to go with you this afternoon—or anytime— Mr. Seaton. For one thing, a beach house hardly seems an *appropriate* place for business. And, for another, I do not appreciate being discussed as though I'm not here!" With hands on her hips, she finished, "And, furthermore, I don't even know what work you have in mind."

"You're quite right," Mr. Seaton said, a hint of humor playing around his dark eyes. "I can see, Miss O'Shea, that your temper matches your hair."

"Really?" Candle shot back. "Judging from the way you burst into this office like thunder, I don't wonder that your own hair is so black!"

Mr. Seaton laughed, and the transformation caused Candle's heart to skip a beat. "I apologize, Miss O'Shea. For thundering. I am, as you've probably guessed, in a rush—though that doesn't excuse my rudeness. As for the beach house, its walls offer me something my office in Lakemont does not—privacy and quiet. My regular secretary can't leave her work, and I need someone to help me finish my doctoral thesis—someone who's willing to work long hours for ample pay. Therefore, it's imperative that I have a serious-minded individual interested in *work,* not me."

Candle couldn't let that pass. "You flatter yourself, Mr. Seaton!"

"Do I?" He frowned for a moment as though genuinely considering her comment, then shook his head. "I think not. Since my wife died . . ." A vulnerable look flitted across his face. ". . . I've been amazed by the number of attractive women who have made it known that they're available."

"And you're not interested?"

"No, I have work to do, Miss O'Shea, and I need your help."

The last ended with such an appealing plea that Candle found herself taking him seriously at last.

"I'm beginning to understand your predicament, Mr. Seaton. And, to ease your mind, yes, I would welcome concentrated work." Thoughts of escape from her entanglement with Gary made her most convincing. "My experience with the editorial department of Woodward Publishing might be of assistance to you, too."

"See!" Seaton beamed at Mrs. Powers, who, well entertained by this lively conversation, looked as though she were recalling Candle's photograph. "I *knew* this was the woman I'd been looking for!"

"That may be," Candle said, cautious once more, "but are you the employer *I'm* looking for? I certainly don't object to long hours, but where will we work, Mr. Seaton? Surely a beach house would be too, uh, intimate for work late at night."

Noah Seaton chuckled. "Not at all."

Candle wasn't used to being dismissed so lightly. Not that she intended for a moment to chase after this man as others had apparently done, but, neither did she like being treated like a wall fixture!

Mr. Seaton's explanation, however, took another turn. "I would require you to stay at the house until my thesis is finished, Miss O'Shea. But the place isn't small, and under the eye of my housekeeper, the arrangement will be far from intimate."

"I see," Candle said, glad for the burned flush that hid her embarrassment.

"Will you come with me, then?" he asked with a strange mixture of business-like urgency and little-boy appeal. "I give you my word that you'll be provided for and that I'll not be overbearing."

Candle smiled at his rather impish grin. "And, I'm to take you at your word?"

The grin vanished, and Mr. Seaton became serious again. "In my business, Miss O'Shea, my word is usually enough."

"And, what," she finally thought to ask, "is your business?"

Seaton glanced at the highly amused Mrs. Powers, then turned back to Candle.

"I assumed you knew, but, of course, you couldn't. I'm a clergyman, Miss O'Shea."

chapter
2

ON THE WAY BACK TO MARCY'S, Candle wondered if she'd imagined the interview. She certainly felt unreal. Her head throbbed, and each moment brought new agony to her sensitive skin. She wished she could wrap herself in a refrigerated blanket and put her life on hold.

She hoped Marcy would provide refreshing humor as they discussed the events of the morning. But, when she told her friend about the job, Marcy exclaimed, "You're going to do what!"

"Marcy, that doesn't help! Do you have any aspirin?"

While her friend checked the medicine shelf, Candle studied the wardrobe she'd brought. No need to take the green silk or the rust chiffon. The button-front cotton shifts would do, and never mind the belts or sashes.

"Here's your aspirin." Marcy plopped on the edge of the bed while Candle packed. "Now tell me again what you're going to do before I think you've suffered heatstroke."

"I have a job, but I have to move into my employer's beach house. Hand me that jacket, would you?"

Marcy tossed her the jacket. "You can't just move in with a stranger, job or no job!"

"Don't worry. Mr. Seaton isn't the least interested in

women, and certainly not a pathetic-looking creature like me." The words sounded brittle, and Candle licked her puffy lips.

"Honestly, Candle! You won't stay pathetic."

"I certainly hope not, but then Mr. Seaton is apt to think my brain and capabilities have vanished with this burn! Oh, that man makes me angry!" Furiously Candle shook the wrinkles out of her housecoat. Then, refolding it neatly, she set it in her suitcase.

"The more you tell me, the less I understand! In plain English, why are you taking this job?"

"It pays well," Candle called from the closet. "It's something I can do. It's demanding, and, therefore, should help me focus on something besides Gary. And . . ." She'd been about to say that Noah Seaton was intriguing.

"And?"

"I wouldn't mind proving to Mr. Seaton that a woman can be interested in her looks *and* competent!" She disappeared into the bathroom and came back, waving her toothbrush. "You know, Marcy, it'd also be a pleasure to persuade that man that every woman on earth isn't chasing after him!"

"He said that?"

"In so many words, yes."

"Braggart!"

"Not really. That's what's so strange." Candle glanced around the room to see if she'd forgotten anything. "He seems burdened by it." She rechecked an emptied drawer. "He's a minister."

"Oh." Marcy sat, swinging her feet. "Maybe this job isn't totally hopeless. But I'm still disappointed."

"Whatever for?"

"You're leaving, silly! I enjoyed having you around."

Candle squeezed her friend's hands. "Then, you'll have me back when the job ends?"

"Of course," Marcy said warmly. "Do you have any idea how long it will last?"

"A few weeks, I imagine. Mr. Seaton—do you suppose I should call him *Rev.* Seaton?" Candle injected, then dismissed the idea. "Mr. Seaton says he has two ministerial students, his regular secretary, and his assistant taking charge while he's away."

"Away from where?"

"Trinity Church in Lakemont. Do you know where that is?"

"Inland about twenty miles or so," Marcy said. "It's a nice town—I've been through there a couple times—but it's no West Palm."

"What do you mean?"

"It's not so lavish that they could afford to supply their pastor with a beach house."

Candle shrugged. "Maybe he owns it privately."

She glanced around again, noted her makeup case on the bureau, and debated whether to take it. She decided not. If Marcy's predictions were true, the next few days would see her back to normal, and while she didn't plan on using makeup to enhance her looks, neither did she want to use it to hide them. An unflattering hairstyle, unflattering dresses— that would be enough.

On impulse, she asked Marcy, "Remember that tannish-gold dress that was too long for you?"

"The one that looked ghastly when you tried it on?"

Candle nodded. "May I borrow it?"

"But the coloring made you look sick!"

"I know. It may come in handy."

Reluctantly, Marcy got the dress, adding, "You're not acting like yourself—open, honest, truthful—remember? I hope you know what you're doing."

"Me too!" Candle shut the suitcase with a bang. "Can I borrow your car?"

"Oh, brother! Let me guess. Your sports coupe doesn't fit the image of a dowdy but conscientious employee. Right?"

Candle gave her a sheepish look. "Please, Marcy? I didn't plan a deception, but I don't want to jeopardize this job. The man jumped to conclusions, that's all. And, I don't want him to find out his mistake until I'm ready. Is that so dreadful?"

Marcy mumbled something about rationalization then tossed Candle her car keys. "It'll be fun driving your sports coupe instead of my old clunker."

"You are truly a dear."

"I know," Marcy teased. "And I'd give you a good-bye hug, but you'd probably scream. Shouldn't you see a dermatologist?"

Candle gave her friend a quick kiss. "I'll be okay." Then she was off.

From the doorway, Marcy hollered after her. "I hope you're not making a mistake, Candle."

"It's Louise," she called over her shoulder. "If you phone, ask for me by my middle name—okay?"

Marcy clapped a hand to her forehead and groaned. "You *must* be delirious!"

"Maybe so!" Candle blew a kiss, then hopped into Marcy's car, and took off.

The address, scrawled carelessly on the back of Noah Seaton's card, was not difficult to find, once deciphered. But, when she arrived, Candle wasn't sure it was the right place. He'd said the house was large, but she had merely envisioned a bigger version of Marcy's cottage with its weathered cypress and homey charm. What she found, however, was an estate.

Through a cluster of palm trees, a tiled roof shone dully.

Below it, the pink stuccoed walls sprawled, U-shaped, on the close-cropped grass. Azaleas, blooming early in the spring-like weather, displayed lavish dashes of red and pink, while border grass edged the paved driveway like drooping sentries.

As Candle followed the pavement's curve to the back of the house, she saw that the arms of the *U* were enclosed with a high stuccoed wall surrounding a pool and garden. On the second floor of the Spanish house, wrought-iron balconies, set symmetrically on both wings, overlooked the Atlantic.

"Some cottage!" she remarked to herself as she switched off the car's engine.

For a moment, her doubts tugged, and she wondered if she were doing the right thing. Then she remembered her alternatives—waiting until her skin had cleared to find another job, or returning prematurely to Gary. With renewed resolve, she slammed the rusty car door and marched to the nearest entrance.

Her finger poised, mid-air, on its way to the doorbell when the massive, carved oak panels swung open, revealing a woman dressed in black. "Miss O'Shea?"

Dumbly, Candle nodded at the formidable figure.

"Mrs. Cousins," the woman said, by way of introduction. "You're not to use the back door." And, with that welcome, the housekeeper ushered her in.

It didn't surprise Candle that Mrs. Cousins was "no-nonsense"—Noah Seaton wouldn't settle for anything less! But this magnificent house was unexpected, and Candle took it in as she followed the stiff starch and steel-rodded back down the long corridor to a winding stair.

The stairway, railed with a black iron grillwork of a simple pattern, stood, presumably, at the front of the house, across from a grand entranceway. Beautifully carved oak marked the door where Candle should have entered, and in the foyer, a dark red Oriental carpet, muted by years of wear, covered an oblong of parquetry. To the left, stretched a spacious room cluttered with books and a tasteful arrangement of contemporary sofas done in white Italian leather. On the right, the western sun streamed into the dining room and bounced light off a long pink marble table. The straight legs and lines, Candle noted, kept it from being gawdy.

She would have liked to look around, but Mrs. Cousins motioned her up the stairs, and Candle followed with her low heels clicking noisily on the uncarpeted oak. The housekeeper's sensibly wedged shoes moved without a sound until they reached the top when, to Candle's irrational satisfaction, the soles squeaked loudly.

"Your quarters are here, Miss O'Shea." Standing on the upper landing, Mrs. Cousins pointed to the left. "And on the other side . . ."

"Am I."

Candle jumped. Noah Seaton was standing in the doorway, his hand extended. She shook it and was surprised to find his grasp warm.

"Welcome, Miss O'Shea. I assume you and Mrs. Cousins have introduced yourselves."

She nodded, feeling inexplicably shy. This school-girl gaping would have to stop, she told herself firmly.

If Seaton noticed, he didn't let on. Instead, he lifted the suitcase Candle had set at her feet.

"We mustn't leave you standing here in the hallway." Then, turning to Mrs. Cousins, he asked, "Have you had time to ready Miss O'Shea's rooms?"

The plural noun escaped Candle's ears. She'd been watching the housekeeper's face as her employer spoke, and the sudden smile of affection startled her. Perhaps, she decided, Mrs. Cousins was human after all. Maybe their boss was too.

25

With this hopeful thought, Candle tagged along in the direction her employer had taken. Mr. Seaton appeared in the doorway to a room, empty-handed, and, with a note of apology, asked, "Would you mind working on your first day? It is rather late."

"For most people, you mean," she said, and he laughed. His stunning smile quickened her pulse, but she didn't guess that her own was disarming.

He looked at her oddly then, head cocked to one side appraising her, but not awkwardly so. Then, straightening, he resumed a business air. "Is an hour long enough for you to freshen up and unpack?"

"Certainly."

"Then I'll see you in my study in one hour." And with that, he crossed the lengthy hall in rapid strides and disappeared behind a massive door.

Candle stood, watching him go, until Mrs. Cousins cleared her throat.

"Would you like to see your rooms now?"

"Yes," Candle said brightly, entering the quarters in which she'd be staying.

What she saw took her breath away. Centered on the left wall, which divided the bedroom from a sitting room, a high four-poster bed was draped with yards and yards of creamy chiffon, held back with golden cord. Antique white brocade, thickly padded, covered the top frame and matched the tailored bedcover. Beneath it, no doubt, were white satin sheets. Several tufted round pillows rested in creams and whites at the head of the bed, and, outside the chiffon curtain stood a low table of creamy marble. On it, Candle's suitcase looked conspicuously shabby.

Across the room on the opposite wall, a cream-colored dresser stretched out generous drawer space, and above it hung a large gilted mirror. Candle avoided a peek at her reflection and looked, instead, beyond, to a kitchen-sized bath with its adjacent cozy dressing room. A second door, opposite her own entrance to the bathroom was closed, and Candle asked Mrs. Cousins what was beyond.

"Rev. Seaton's bedroom," came the curt reply.

Candle did not think she'd imagined the emphasis on the word *reverend*. "In a house this large, surely we don't share a bath," she countered primly.

"No," Mrs. Cousins answered, motioning Candle to a smaller bath near the door that separated the bedroom from the enormous sitting room. "Do you need help unpacking?"

"Thank you, no," Candle said and was relieved when Mrs. Cousins took this as her cue to leave.

Alone, she slipped off her shoes and curled her bare toes into the plush cream carpet extending throughout the rooms. She supposed she should unpack, but instead she inspected the sitting room, where she'd probably spend much of her time.

A quick look in the long L-shaped desk showed it to be well-stocked with typing supplies and the best equipment, including an intercom. But the desk's sleek metal lines clashed with the white wicker and multicolored floral cushions of the otherwise well-decorated room.

At the end of the work area, a padded chaise with an accompanying table stood in front of double glass doors that led onto one of the balconies Candle had spotted from the driveway. Flower pots stood around, and indoors, beside the lighted panes, a cart spilled with begonias and a variety of ferns whose arms entangled themselves beneath the shade of a potted fan palm.

From the windowed doors, the view of the ocean was magnificent, and for a moment Candle watched the waves crashing ashore. Already she loved this cheery room.

Reluctantly, she turned back to the task at hand. She had less than an hour to tend her flushed skin and unpack her dresses before the wrinkles set. She was debating about which to do first in the short time allotted when she noticed the painting hanging on the wall opposite her desk. Stepping into the center of the room for a better look, she gasped at a portrait of the most gorgeous woman she'd ever seen.

The beautiful eyes stared back. From the larger-than-life canvas, the woman seemed to follow Candle's movements. Sulky, sultry, the lower lip protruded in a slight pout that seemed to say, "Come here" and "Don't you dare," all at the same time. Clusters of white-blonde curls saucily topped the pretty head, and ringlets draped against a long and slender neck. Apparently, this room over which the eyes stood sentry had been hers.

Feeling like an intruder, Candle hurried into the smaller bath and closed the door. The mirrored portrait that greeted her was far different from the canvased beauty, and Candle gave a little shriek of dismay. If possible, her skin had reddened more throughout the day, giving her a scalded, fevered look. Until then, it had not occurred to her that she might actually be ill. She'd merely thought to endure the discomfort until it went away.

Still feeling the interloper, she rummaged through the medicine cabinet, and found, then swallowed, another aspirin. The cool shower had helped earlier, so she now stripped off her smock and stepped into the marble-edged tub.

She let the cold water pour over her as long as she dared, then wrapped herself in a thick white towel and padded across the carpet to her suitcase. By the time she'd donned a lightweight sleeveless smock and put away her things, she'd convinced herself that she was fine, that her reflection in the mirror was simply a pitiful contrast to the lovely portrait.

Besides, hadn't the Lord used her dreadful appearance to land this job? Candle thought so, and, therefore, she could hardly complain.

Hour up, she arrived somewhat breathless at the door of Noah Seaton's study. Her tap met with an immediate response, and Candle had the distinct impression he'd been pacing.

With nerves still on edge from the sun, the portrait, and now his presence, Candle was relieved to hear familiar sounds coming from Seaton's study.

She clapped her hands. "Schubert's Serenade!"

He smiled. "You won't mind my keeping the stereo on while we work?"

"Not at all."

"Then let's begin," he said, motioning her into the room.

A large, oak-paneled leather-topped desk, stacked high with paper and the clutter of busyness, sat on the south wall, and in a nearby corner, a smaller desk bore a typewriter like the one in the sitting room.

At the eastern end of Seaton's study, which overlooked the ocean from the second balcony, a button-tufted, blue-gray leather sofa faced a pair of matching wingbacks. A heavy, dark-stained table completed the arrangement. On its glass top sat another stack of papers and a tape recorder. In this cozy area, Seaton told Candle to make herself comfortable, not realizing that was impossible.

When they'd seated themselves, he thrust an outline of his manuscript into her hands. Candle took it, scanning it with interest. At the top of the first page, he'd written the title of his thesis, "The Variations of Personalities of the Individual Denominations of Christianity," then crossed out the word *Individual*. The change brought a smile to her lips as she read on.

29

Because she had deciphered his scrawling hand earlier, Candle had little trouble now. The basic outline of the thesis contained innumerable corrections, hastily made, as though he didn't want to forget some important point. Candle read through the scribbles, concentrating on the purpose of the work. Its theme of church unity amidst diversity intrigued her, and she became so engrossed in the information that she momentarily forgot his presence.

"What do you think?" he asked when she'd finished reading.

"It's quite good. Really!"

He rewarded her with a slow smile. "You sound surprised, Miss O'Shea."

"Sorry. I certainly didn't underestimate you. I mean, I . . ." she fumbled awkwardly for words. Why must this man make her so ill at ease? She took in a deep breath, and, somewhat composed, tried again. "One doesn't expect the *outline* of a thesis to be so interesting."

He grinned. "Probably not. I trust, then, that you won't be bored."

"That's unlikely." She smiled back. She could see herself being tongue-tied for weeks, but bored? Never!

"Have you found *your* denominational personality?" he asked lightly, but the question troubled her. When she didn't answer, he added, "I'm only teasing, Miss O'Shea."

She wished for a moment that she could let his statement pass as he'd meant it to, but her conscience unloosened her tongue. "I should tell you, Mr. Seaton, that I'm not a churchgoer. My close relationship with God doesn't depend on going to church." There. She'd said it without adding more to the day's regrets.

"Your church affiliation, or in this case, your lack of it, was not a qualification for the job," he answered dryly.

"I appreciate that. But, well . . . I should tell you that I left the church because I haven't found it to be what it should." Now she wondered if she'd gone too far.

He settled back in his chair. "What *should* the church be, Miss O'Shea?"

She glanced at him and, satisfied that he honestly wanted her opinion, answered. "It's easier for me to say what it should *not* be."

"Go on."

"I believe that the church should not be prejudicial, bigoted, judgmental, unloving—"

"I agree," he interrupted, leaning forward. "That's one of the reasons I chose this particular topic for my research."

"Really?" She was surprised by his admission. "Then let's get started, shall we?"

Candle reached for a notepad, and he started dictating. He spoke slowly and clearly, but without stopping, and Candle only paused in her notetaking when he got up from the wingback and began to pace.

She wouldn't have minded pacing herself. The blue-gray leather stuck uncomfortably to her red skin, and she scooted forward, perching on the studded edge. After a few minutes in this strained position, she leaned back and immediately felt the rush of warmth from her own skin enveloping her like a winter mitten. She tried not to squirm, but eventually her movements, not unlike that of a restless child, caught his attention.

"Is something wrong, Miss O'Shea?"

"Oh, no," she said, trying not to move under his questioning stare. Then, "It's just that I have a little sunburn." The confession relieved her more than she'd expected.

"So that's what's the matter! I'd wondered if you had a chronic problem—" He stopped himself just short of rudeness. "But now that you've told me, I can see you have quite a bit more than a 'little' sunburn! A friend of mine can tell us what to do. He's not a dermatologist, but . . ."

"Please! I'm fine," Candle insisted as he reached for the desk phone. "Let's keep working."

"I promised I wouldn't be overbearing, Miss O'Shea, but it somehow seems inhumane to keep going."

"Then I'm sorry I told you," she snapped. "You hired someone to do a job for you, and that's what I'm trying to do!"

"Very well." He began once more to dictate. But his jaw tightened, and his voice seemed strained.

As he paced, talking, Noah Seaton's long strides quickened, back and forth, back and forth, back and forth. Candle's head throbbed to the faster tempo, and she could barely keep up with his speedy dictation. His thoughts seemed to rush out with frenzied haste, and his voice swelled with the crescendo of the background music playing on the stereo. Then, when Candle thought she could stand it no longer, he suddenly broke off, and the silence was louder than a crash.

"That's enough, Miss O'Shea." She'd been about to tell him the same thing! "Here are the tapes I dictated before your arrival. Here are the notes for insertion, and here are the first few pages I've written by hand. Dinner is at seven." And with that, he strode out of the room and down the stairs, leaving her alone in his study.

Oh, that man can be infuriating! Candle thought. It didn't matter that he was right, or even that he was trying to be thoughtful. She would not have him thinking her a fluff brain for staying out in the sun!

Gathering up the outline, notes, and tapes, she stormed back to her room and began work immediately on inserting the various changes he'd indicated. She assimilated the

32

material in a logical order, glad for the spacious desk on which to arrange the papers in proper sequence. Then she set about typing the final copy with swollen fingers.

Minutes flew along with the machine's daisy wheel, and Candle soon produced a stack of neat, finished copy. While she worked, she shut out all other thoughts, and so the sudden rap on the hallway door to the sitting room startled her.

Candle opened the door a crack and saw Mrs. Cousins bearing a look of disapproval and a tray.

"Rev. Seaton told me to bring this up to you," the housekeeper said through pinched lips. Without such an order it was clear that she would have done otherwise.

Totally out of synch with time, Candle glanced at her watch aghast. It was well past eight, and she wondered what the reverend would think of her now!

"Mrs. Cousins! I'm so sorry! I lost track of time."

The housekeeper sniffed. "Seems so. In the future, let me know if you don't intend to come down to dinner."

"But I . . ." Candle stopped herself. There was no point in arguing. "I will. And thank you for the tray."

She started to close the door then, but Mrs. Cousins detained her. "Rev. Seaton also asked about your health."

"Tell him I'm fine, please," Candle said, then shut the door before the housekeeper could witness her sudden flow of tears.

This is ridiculous, she told herself. But ridiculous or not, she couldn't stop the gentle weeping until the day's frustrations had unleashed themselves.

Food had no appeal, but she investigated the contents of the tray she'd set on a corner of her desk. White grapes, a variety of cheeses, and wafers of wheat hid under aluminum covers, and a silver carafe held pink lemonade. Thirsty, she drank two tumblers and sipped a third.

In a crystal bud vase stood a long-stemmed rose, appropriately shaded in a deep-flushed pink, and beneath it, someone had placed an envelope. Candle opened it to a message penned in that now familiar hand.

Medical instructions! She read them quickly with ambivalent feelings jerking at her. *How dare he!* she thought. Then, just as rapidly, she praised him for going ahead and calling his doctor friend without her permission.

Admittedly, her condition needed attention whether she liked it or not. Marcy was right after all. She'd had an allergic reaction to the sun, and the effects of her burn had set in more gradually. No wonder she'd felt worse throughout the day.

Candle slid her fingers underneath the edges of the covered plates on her tray and pulled out a small pill bottle containing an antihistamine and a tube of topical dressing. Although she'd felt feverish earlier, she now shivered slightly and decided to dispense with another cool shower. She rose from her desk, satisfied that she'd done enough work for one day, then sat down abruptly until a wave of lightheadedness passed.

Feeling foolish, she made her way slowly into the bathroom where she disrobed, then smeared the ointment over her damaged skin. She swallowed the antihistamine, downing it with one full glass of water, then another, supposing vaguely that she was a bit dehydrated.

Moving through a fog, she had enough presence of mind to think, *I can't get this sticky ointment on those satin sheets!* Then, with arms and legs well-covered, she crawled into bed, shivering uncontrollably.

Chilled, she fell into a restless sleep. Then later she tossed off her covers, feverish again. Back and forth she went between the two extremes, and in her dreams, a figure paced.

Hot. So hot. But her forehead felt strangely cold, icy. She

tried to waken, but the antihistamine had added drowsiness to her exhaustion. And so she slept.

When morning came, sunlight from the eastern windows nudged her into consciousness, and she stretched her sore arms, feeling reasonably rested and suddenly alert.

The first thing she noticed was that she'd left the drapes undrawn. And the second was that, on the nightstand beside her, a folded washcloth lay damp on a bucket of melting ice.

chapter
3

SOMEONE WAS HERE! The thought hit her, and she bolted upright. Then, feeling giddy, she sank back against the down-filled pillows. What a mess she'd gotten herself into! And, undoubtedly, she realized with a shudder, Noah Seaton felt the same.

She couldn't stay here, she thought helplessly, but neither could she leave. As she wrestled with this dilemma, a light knock on the bedroom door attracted her attention.

"Come in," she called and was immediately relieved to see Mrs. Cousins, rather than her employer, peering in.

"You're awake."

"Yes."

"I s'pose you'll want breakfast."

Candle's stomach rumbled a reply, but she thought she'd rather starve than ask the housekeeper to bring her another tray. Fortunately, she had to do neither.

"Rev. Seaton said you were ill, and I wasn't to bother you until you'd waked on your own."

So he had been the one who'd tended her during the night! And she'd thought she'd been dreaming! Embarrassed now, she recognized the situation as a nightmare. How would she ever face him?

"Where is he? Mr. Seaton, I mean."

"Called away. Some emergency. They just won't leave the poor man alone!" Mrs. Cousins said with more emotion than Candle had yet witnessed from her.

She supposed that the "they" meant the people of his church, but considering last night's events, Candle knew, to her shame, that "they" included her.

"When will he return?" she asked now.

"This afternoon, I expect. Meanwhile, I'm to bring your meals and see that you rest. Rev. Seaton's orders."

"Mrs. Cousins, I truly am sorry for this inconvenience—"

"Might've told us you were ill," the housekeeper chided, then disappeared.

She came back moments later with a breakfast tray, which she placed, like a tiny wicker table, across Candle's lap. Propped up in bed, Candle tried to lighten the awkward situation by saying, "I can't recall the last time I had breakfast in bed!" to which the housekeeper replied, "Hmmpf."

"Thank you," she called as Mrs. Cousins turned to go, then muttered, "Grouch," as the door closed.

Candle sighed. She had to admit that she'd done nothing to help Mrs. Cousins's disposition, and she did appreciate the woman's loyal service to a man who obviously needed her as a buffer. She wondered idly what emergency had called him, then, reminding herself that it was none of her business, she attacked her food.

Piping hot eggs, scrambled with bits of bacon, onion, and cheese curled on one platter, accompanied by a small bowl of white grits in a pool of butter. Slices of cool melon, honeydew and cantaloupe, curved in another bowl, and a saucer of golden toast was surrounded by jams and jellies. Simple fare, but well-suited for one who hadn't eaten since yesterday's lunch.

Appreciatively, Candle ate until she'd emptied every dish and drained the tumbler of freshly-squeezed orange juice. Then she set the tray aside. She got up slowly, not wanting to topple under another wave of lightheadedness, but the hearty meal had done its job. The giddiness was gone.

She felt, in fact, remarkably better all over. Last night's sleep and medication had left her pink but far less swollen, and she found she could move about reasonably well. But today, she vowed, she would not push herself beyond sensible limits.

Not wanting to be disturbed, she set the breakfast tray in the hallway outside her door, then carried the carafe of coffee to the small round table overlooking the ocean. A few joggers and shell seekers peopled the shore, which stretched in either direction as far as she could see. Above the gentle waves, a pelican glided lazily, then with a sudden plunge, dove into the water, and came up with bulging pouch.

Enjoying the view, Candle switched on the radio beside her elbow and jiggled the knob until she'd found a classical music station. The melodious strains of "Jesu, Joy of Man's Desiring" swept into the room. *Bach!*

Brad!

"Oh, no!" she cried.

She'd completely forgotten the Bach concert, and after Brad had gone to so much trouble too! The least she could have done was call to beg off. She'd certainly meant to, but the chaotic day and night . . . *No,* she scolded herself, *there was no excuse!* She'd acted like a fluff brain! The thought depressed her.

Hurriedly, Candle freshened up and dressed, her skin sticky again with another application of ointment. According to the instructions she'd been given, she was to take another antihistamine, but the prospect of being drowsy again

38

stopped her. She'd take it after lunch, she decided, and enjoy a nap when the work was done.

Meanwhile, she wanted to catch Marcy at the office. She punched the buttons on the desk phone, and tapping her fingers impatiently, waited for someone to answer.

"M. J. Advertising," came the receptionist's voice. Then, "One moment, please," as Candle waited for Marcy to come on the line.

"Thank goodness, you're there!"

"H'm, excuse me, ma'am, but am I speaking with Louise O'Shea or Candle?"

"Oh, Marcy, I'm sorry," Candle said. "I'd meant to ask if you'd mind filling in for me last night with Brad. Will you forgive me?"

"That depends," Marcy baited, "on whether or not I have your permission for other nights."

"You two hit it off! I knew you would!" Candle said, delighted. "And, yes! You have my permission."

Marcy breathed an audibly exaggerated sigh of relief. "I'd hoped you'd say that. That's why I've already told him I'd go out tonight."

"Marcy! That's great."

"Well, I figured you weren't too serious about him to forget him so readily."

"True."

"Since you're handing out old boyfriends, how about Gary? May I have him too?"

Candle laughed. "Sure, if you promise not to do him bodily harm."

"Impossible! How about your Rev. Seaton then?"

Candle's smile vanished. "Why do I have a feeling that I've just been put through a test?"

"Sorry. I couldn't resist. You did rush out of here in a hurry."

"True again, but if you keep this up, I'm going to call Brad and tell him you scorched me with a sunlamp!"

"Don't you dare!" Marcy laughed. "You *are* okay, aren't you?"

"I'm fine." She mentioned the medication and its effect, omitting her employer's night-long vigil.

The two friends chatted a few minutes more before returning to work. Since Candle had finished typing the revised outline the night before, she now transcribed a tape. This, however, proved difficult to do since her employer had failed to indicate paragraphing. If only she had a word processor, she could move passages about, changing paragraph breaks readily.

Rats!

Candle ripped an uncorrectable sheet out of the typewriter and tossed the wad into the wastebasket. This primitive method of working frustrated her, and she decided to speak to Mr. Seaton about it.

Although she wouldn't admit it, she was bothered most by the deep, melodic voice coming from the tape. His voice. It held such warmth, such passion. And both, she realized glumly, were directed toward his subject matter—the church.

She wished her own experiences had not given her such a jaundiced view. Until she'd met Noah Seaton she'd dismissed the church as an irrelevant part of her life. On this at least she and Gary agreed! But of what value was that common ground for marriage?

Not wanting to think about Gary, Candle shook her head and tried to redirect her rambling thoughts. At this rate, she'd get nothing done all morning.

"Very inefficient, Miss O'Shea," she told herself. And with that in mind, she revised her system, rapidly typing a rough draft of the tape. Later, she could edit the copy and allow for changes before typing the final draft. Not the most desirable system, but it would have to do.

As her fingers flew across the keyboard, the sun left the eastern windows and hovered over the Spanish house. So intent was she upon her work that she didn't hear the knock on her door. And when Mrs. Cousins suddenly stood over her with a lunch tray, she looked up, surprised.

"What do you think you're doing?" the housekeeper fussed.

"Work?" she timidly responded.

"You were told to rest."

Candle sighed. She refused to be intimidated by Mrs. Cousins's caustic tongue, yet she didn't want an enemy either. *Lord, help this woman see we're on the same side!*

"Mrs. Cousins, I know I've been an awful bother to you, and you're only trying to do your job, but so am I! Mr. Seaton has a large amount of work to do in a short time, and even then, he's met with interruptions! The fact that I've slowed him down does not make me feel better. So now I've all this work to catch up. Please don't stop me from doing what I've been hired to do!"

"Hmmpf. As if I could."

Candle smiled. "That's right. You can't stop me. And if Mr. Seaton doesn't like it, he can be annoyed with me. Not you."

"He probably will be, you know."

"I'll risk it."

The housekeeper's mask of disapproval cracked slightly, and Candle thought she caught a glimpse of a smile. But now Mrs. Cousins was speaking to her firmly. "It won't do to overtire and have another bad night."

"I know."

"Did you take your medicine?"

Candle looked sheepish. "I will, I promise. But it makes me drowsy, and a nap can wait until I've finished this." She motioned to the tape on the cassette player.

41

"All right. But don't forget. And, in the meantime, eat your lunch."

"Why, Mrs. Cousins! You're a mother hen."

The lined face wrinkled in an unfamiliar smile then vanished as the housekeeper left Candle alone with her meal. It was delicious! And Candle enjoyed the tiny sandwiches and sliced fruit more, knowing Mrs. Cousins was not the enemy she'd imagined.

By midafternoon, one tape had been transcribed, and Candle debated whether or not to begin another. No, she'd given her word not to overdo—not just to Mrs. Cousins, but to herself. Obediently, she took her medication, then plumping the pillows against the padded headboard, she propped herself in bed. The rough draft she'd typed balanced on her knees, and she expertly penciled in the needed editorial marks until her eyes blurred. Then setting the work aside, she promptly fell asleep.

When she awoke, it was dark, and for one terrible moment she feared she'd re-ignited Mrs. Cousins's wrath by missing dinner. The clock on the nightstand, however, reassured her that it was just past six. Time enough to make herself presentable. Well, she thought wryly, as presentable as she could.

She wondered if her employer had returned, and if so, would he be relieved or irritated by the amount of work she'd accomplished? Probably both. Still, she wished it'd been more, and she thought once again of the word processor.

Dressing with care, Candle quickly discarded the idea of wearing Marcy's tannish-gold and opted instead for an emerald, cotton dress that toned down her skin while highlighting her light green eyes. It wouldn't do to look ill, and she could see for herself that her appearance today was an improvement over yesterday. She twirled in front of the mirror, then deciding that the belt delineated her figure too much, she took it off. It was uncomfortable anyway.

Trembling at the prospect of seeing her employer, Candle headed for the stairs. Halfway down, she met Mrs. Cousins, who was starting up with a tray.

"I'd meant to catch you before you went to any trouble," Candle apologized.

"This is for the reverend. Since he didn't expect you down, he said he'd eat in his study. I'll ask what he wants to do."

The housekeeper had continued climbing the steps as she talked, and without waiting for Candle's reply, she marched down the upper hall. Then reappearing, she motioned Candle to the pastor's study.

"Rev. Seaton said you're to join him," Mrs. Cousins said when Candle hesitated on the landing. "Go on now. I'll bring you a tray shortly."

"Don't you think it's a bit too chummy to dine this way?"

Mrs. Cousins softly chuckled. "No need to worry about that. Now go on," she said again, then added more firmly, "He's tired. Don't either of you work too long."

"We won't," Candle assured her, then impulsively patted the older woman's arm.

He did look tired, she thought, as she entered the room. Without looking up from his desk, he'd called her to come in, and she'd noticed a slight sag in those broad shoulders. Now he glanced up, and as he did so, one dark eyebrow raised as he inspected her.

"You certainly look better," he said at last.

"You don't." Her comment was out before she could stop it. "I mean . . . It's just that . . ." She took a calming breath. "It might be best if you retire early and get a fresh start in the morning."

"Ah. Your concern for my health is touching, Miss O'Shea,

43

but I wonder that you have none for your own. Mrs. Cousins tells me that you've accomplished wonders today, but I must admit I caught you napping when I went to check for myself."

"Really, Mr. Seaton. Despite the fact that you're my employer and that this is your home and that you're a minister of God—"

"That's three facts."

"—stay out of my room!"

"Do you like it?"

"What?"

"Your room."

"Of course. The rooms are wonderful, and you're wonderful for taking such good care of me last night—even though I'd behaved rather childishly in refusing a doctor's advice."

The eyebrow arched again. Whatever did she mean, calling him wonderful?

He was staring at her with those dark eyes when Mrs. Cousins set down a dinner tray then slipped out. Candle wondered what to say, but Noah solved the problem for her by asking if she'd had any difficulty working with the tapes.

"Not really. But without paragraphing and punctuation, the transcribing is tedious. Have you thought about purchasing a word processor?"

He waved a hand, dismissing the idea. "I have no use for one after this project is finished. My secretary at Trinity already has one that she's unable to loan. But you do have a point, Miss O'Shea. In the future, I'll see to it that I indicate every bracket, every comma, every dot."

He was teasing her, and she knew it, but she blurted out, "I'm trying to save you time, not add to your work!"

A corner of his mouth curled in a most disarming way. "I appreciate that, Miss O'Shea." He rose from his desk chair then, indicating that they would dine on the sofa. "I'd prefer the balcony," he said, "but it's chilly at night this time of year."

"I love the view from the sitting room," Candle said, then stopped. All day she'd ignored the eyes of the beautiful portrait that bore holes in her back, but now she asked, "Who's the lovely woman in the painting?"

A frown flitted across his face. "Tasmine. My wife."

Candle had thought as much. Awkwardly, she hurried on. "She had wonderful taste. The bedroom is so elegant, and the cozy sitting room—"

"I'm glad you like them," he interrupted. "But Tasmine would never want credit for those rooms. She detested them." He broke off suddenly as though he'd said too much.

So that was why he'd asked if I liked her rooms, Candle thought. She'd assumed he was being polite. But now it seemed he cared about her approval of his taste, and that speculation filled her with an odd sense of pleasure.

They ate in silence while Candle wondered about Tasmine. If she'd truly despised her quarters, then the only clue to her personality was the low-cut bodice in the portrait, the pouting lip, and mass of curls. Fluff? No, that was unfair, Candle decided. She had no right to confine anyone to a convenient label.

"About that word processor," Candle attempted one more time. "Why don't you rent one? It could save hours, and that alone would be worth the expense—especially if you have many more interruptions like you did today."

"If so, I'll reconsider," he promised. "However, my staff is quite capable of running interference for me."

"Would they dare be otherwise?" she teased.

"Probably not," he agreed good-naturedly.

Their eyes met, sharing humor, then abruptly Candle looked away. This job would be so much easier, she told herself, if she didn't find this man so unbearably attractive. It was worse, however, knowing that the feeling could not possibly be mutual—under the circumstances. She sighed, reminding herself that her unfortunate appearance had gotten her this job, and with God's help, would allow her to keep it until she'd proved herself capable.

Her employer stared at her with a strange expression, and to turn his attentions away from her, Candle asked with genuine interest, "Were you always drawn to the ministry?"

A flicker, a wince, and he shook his head. "A fireman, perhaps, or a motorcycle cop, but a minister? Never!" She rewarded him with a smile. "Actually, I'd expected to take over Seaton Industries," he added, and Candle gave a small gasp.

She hadn't made the connection even though Marcy had mentioned wanting the company's advertising account. His connection with the respected firm, important to the state's economy, certainly explained Noah Seaton's financial means. Why hadn't Marcy thought of that? Or perhaps she had?

"My degree was in business," Noah Seaton went on, "and I did work for my father for a time. But my life felt empty. Now it doesn't," he finished abruptly.

Unable to think of anything else to say, Candle noted, "I doubt you have time for emptiness."

"True enough, but I assure you, Miss O'Shea, my work means more to me than filling time."

"Of course!" she hastily agreed. "It's just that . . . I mean . . ." Oh, he'd made her tongue-tied again! She slowed and ended lamely, "People need you."

He smiled. "Yes. Even in the middle of the night," he said playfully.

Candle supposed she'd asked for that, but next he'd be telling her she snored! "I appreciate your . . . your thoughtfulness, and I'm sure your church does too, Mr. Seaton."

"It's Noah," he said after a moment of silence that was, for her anyway, uncomfortable. His next words, however, made her more so. "May I call you Louise?"

"No!" She hadn't meant to sound so vehement about it, and now he looked at her quizzically. She flushed beneath the stare. "Mr. Seaton—"

"Noah."

"Noah." She moistened her lips. "Louise is my middle name."

The thick eyebrows raised, but he waited for her to go on.

"Well, you . . . you made such a thing about exotic names that I couldn't very well . . . My first name is Candle." She ended with a touch of defiance in her voice.

To her surprise, her employer threw back his head, laughing. But even though she was relieved, Candle didn't find anything so amusing.

"I'm sorry, Miss O'Shea. Candle," he said. "It's a fitting name. Utilitarian, actually."

Utilitarian!

"Descriptive," he amended as though he'd sensed her displeasure. "Or at least, I'm sure it will be when that sunburn fades."

Alone later in her room, Candle thought of Noah's extraordinary response to her name and couldn't decide if she were pleased or not. One good thing, she thought as she readied herself for bed—he hadn't automatically considered her a rag-mop brain!

Heading for the marble bath, Candle paused before the glamorous portrait in the sitting room. Tasmine. The hauntingly exotic name fit, and Candle couldn't help but wonder if Noah's wife appreciated his decision to go into the ministry.

"You're jumping to conclusions," she chided herself. "And on appearances!"

Tasmine was really none of her business. But as she turned away from the gorgeous face, Candle wondered at the small fist of jealousy that knotted her stomach as she thought of those eyes behind her, following.

chapter
4

WHEN CANDLE AWOKE THE NEXT MORNING still thinking about Tasmine, she flung the silky covers over her pink face and groaned. *Okay, I'm jealous!* she admitted. *Please help me get my mind off her, Lord!*

The morning's work soon took care of that as she and Noah pored over the notes he'd been accumulating for months. With obvious care and accuracy, he'd noted both general facts and intriguing details that breathed life into the dry subject matter. On each index card, he'd written down the title, author, and page number of his source. His own thoughts had been kept separate, usually dictated into his tape recorder, but sometimes hastily jotted on small cards. The results were a half dozen or so stacks of index cards, each a few inches high.

At first glance, Candle was impressed by the amount of tedious, thorough work Noah had done. At second glance, she was dismayed.

"Noah, I don't know how to tell you this," she hesitantly began, "but from what I can see, these cards are not divided according to topics. Take this one, for example." She picked up a card she'd just put down. "Your notes cover church politics in Rome, the humanists of the Renaissance, and an amusing legend about a woman and her beehive—all on one card!"

"You don't appreciate the story about the honeycomb shaped like a cathedral?"

Candle smiled. "It's not that. It's just that honeycombs and church politics don't mix! Sorting them out could be *sticky* business."

Noah laughed. "Any suggestions?"

She thought a moment. "It's too early for me to tell yet. . . . I mean, I don't know your material enough to say—it's possible that I can color-code the basic categories of information."

"Yellow for honeycombs?" he teased.

"Something like that. I'm sure I can devise a workable system for underlining, and then we can easily see which card goes where."

"Except that some cards will go in more than one stack."

"Yes," Candle admitted, "but with your outline as a guide, I can assign each color a numerical sequence for its use in the thesis. Then, when you've finished pulling notes from one color stack, I can sort the cards into the next color to be used."

Noah didn't say anything. He just stared at her, and Candle felt as though he were seeing her for the first time. His dark eyes reflected admiration. Yet they were also unnerving.

"Perhaps," he said at last, "you can see why I surround myself with an efficient staff."

Candle smiled, not trusting herself to say anything. Moments before she'd begun to relax in his laughter, but now she wasn't at all sure this subtle change of mood was funny.

For a while they worked quietly, with Candle concentrating on the topical sequence in Noah's outline, while he assessed the file cards. Occasionally she glanced up to catch him frowning.

"This is going to take more work than you hired on to do."

"I don't mind," Candle assured him.

"What about your work at Woodward Publishing?"

"It'll still be there."

He studied her quizzically. "Is your personal life so uninvolved that you can take a week—maybe two—longer than intended?"

"That's really not your concern as long as I do the job. I've already told you I would," Candle answered with a coolness she didn't feel. "Keeping one's word is not confined to clerical collars, is it?"

"I suppose not," he mumbled, then they both went back to work.

After that exchange, however, it was hard for her to keep her mind on what she was doing. Like an instant replay, her thoughts went over and over the morning's conversation, trying to find some clue that would explain Noah's attitude toward her. Was he offended by her assessment of his index cards? No, she didn't think so. Maybe he didn't want her around longer than he'd expected. But, no, he would've jumped at her suggestion about renting a computer if he'd wanted her gone quickly. Money was no problem. But something was, and for the life of her, Candle couldn't figure it out.

Finally she decided to ask. When he rose from his desk to pour himself a fresh cup of coffee, Candle said, "Is something the matter?"

He gave her a blank look. "Why?"

She shrugged. "You seem like . . . like something's bothering you."

"Do I?" Politely he raised the silver carafe in her direction. "Coffee?"

She shook her head. "One cup is my limit."

"It's decaffeinated. Mrs. Cousins's orders."

51

With a light chuckle, Candle held out her cup.

She thought he'd avoided answering her, but when he'd seated himself again, Noah said, "I suppose something is bothering me, Candle, but it's nothing that time won't resolve. Meanwhile, I hope it suffices to say—your abilities are . . ." He hesitated. ". . . appreciated."

His words warmed her, yet she felt a light chill, more goose bumpy than ominous, and after that, the hours flew by.

The next few days flew, too—each settling into its own pattern, depending upon the work Noah had for her to do. Some mornings Candle stayed in the sunroom, typing up the thoughts he had dictated on tape, unless he called her on the intercom to come into his study. But she much preferred his company to the silent portrait looking over her—looking down.

In the evenings she escaped Tasmine's sultry stare by taking leisurely walks on the beach, but Noah never joined her. Instead, he took his exercise in the pool—where Candle was not about to join him! She'd packed her swimming suit—a pink one-piece—but she'd yet to use it. She supposed it'd be safe enough after he'd gone inside, but she wasn't ready to take that plunge. Her figure was certainly not one that he'd describe as "matronly."

The careless cotton dresses had done their job of hiding her attractiveness while the antihistamine had worked to reveal it. By the end of the week, only traces of puffiness remained around her eyes, and most of the rash had disappeared. Her pink skin had not begun to peel, but all in all, she didn't look too bad—which *was* too bad, Candle thought!

She needed more time. Time to prove herself. Time to show him she could be trusted. Time for him to accept her for herself—despite appearances.

That his own appearance caused her heart to flutter bothered Candle. She could see why women pursued him, but it disturbed her that persons of her gender had gotten under his skin without really seeing underneath it! Had no one except Mrs. Cousins noticed the warm, intelligent, caring person beneath that handsome exterior? Did no one value his mental attributes? His spiritual strengths? His humor?

Candle sighed. Trinity Church undoubtedly accepted the fine person Noah was, but that seemed a poor substitute for a personal relationship. Yet Noah had made it clear from the beginning that he was not at all interested in a romantic encounter. He was her employer. Nothing more.

Sitting alone on a Sunday afternoon in Noah's dead wife's rooms was doing nothing for Candle's frame of mind. According to Mrs. Cousins, Noah had driven over to Lakemont for the weekend, and she had no idea when he'd be back. Candle felt peeved that he hadn't mentioned his plans to her, and the last thing she wanted to do was sit around, waiting.

The endless stacks of paper on her desk tempted her to occupy her time and thoughts with work, but she knew she'd be fresher—more efficient—if she took a break from routine. Picking up a pen, she started a letter to Gary before deciding she had nothing to say to him. She wadded up the parchment Noah had thoughtfully left for her personal use and aimed it toward the wastebasket. She missed, and Tasmine's smirk seemed to say, "I knew you would."

The walls of the spacious room closed in tight, and Candle felt an urge to flee. Grabbing her purse and Marcy's car keys, she hurried down the stairs, and with a "See you later" to Mrs. Cousins, she ran out the door. It would suit her fine if Noah came back before she did and wondered where *she* was.

With windows rolled against a sudden shower, the car put Candle on slow bake as she headed toward the beach cottage. She hoped Marcy would be home. All week she'd meant to check back with her friend during office hours but had used work as an excuse during the day and Marcy's lack of a home phone during the night. The truth was—she hadn't really wanted to talk to anyone. Not even Marcy. Thoughts of Noah Seaton seemed too private to discuss.

She wondered if Marcy felt the same way about Brad. *Oh, I hope so!* she thought. And then she wondered what way that was.

When she arrived at the cottage, however, her sports car was gone with no signs of life around. She pounded on the door, calling Marcy's name, but no answer.

Getting back into the old clunker, she drove through the beach town nearby and browsed through a few small shops, killing time. Then feeling hungry, she remembered she'd skipped lunch, much to Mrs. Cousins's chagrin. To avoid vexing her further, Candle dropped a coin in a pay phone and informed the housekeeper she wouldn't be home for dinner, but she carefully avoided clues to her whereabouts or questions about Noah's return. Hanging up the phone, she felt pleased, despite the fact that she'd be dining alone.

Since Highway A1A connected one small beach town to another, Candle drove down it, keeping watch for any restaurant she'd heard Brad or Marcy mention. A cozy place overlooking the ocean, with its offer of fresh seafood and steaks, appealed to her, so she pulled into the paved drive and cut the spewing engine. Marcy really could use a tune-up. Vowing to take care of that for her during the next uneventful weekend, Candle went inside.

The expected sea motif greeted her along with a smiling hostess who seated Candle, as she'd requested, at a corner table overlooking the ocean. Settled in, she turned down the offer of a before-dinner drink and asked for a menu instead. As she scanned the entrées, she felt eyes staring at her. Curious, she looked up.

From the nearby bar, a very tanned young man with thick sun-bleached hair lifted his glass to her. Politely, Candle returned his smile then gave her full attention to the debate at hand—charbroiled marlin or fresh catfish. Both sounded wonderfully delicious.

"Have you ever tried marlin?" someone standing over her asked, and Candle discovered the young man had crossed to her corner as though he were planning to stay. "It's good— and I'm not big on fish." As he spoke, his drink sloshed slightly.

Candle closed the menu. "Thanks. I'll give it a try." She started to ask if he were a lifeguard but decided that might encourage him.

"You have a nice smile."

"Do I?" she said, automatically rewarding him with another. Then in hopes of dismissing him, she looked out upon the sea.

"Are you eating alone?" he asked, and without turning around, she merely nodded. "I could keep you company," he said, so childlike that Candle couldn't bear to hurt his feelings.

"That's a lovely offer," she said, facing him, "but I really need to be alone tonight. Sorry."

He grinned. "Thinking about some guy, huh?"

She shrugged.

"Well, don't think about him too much. I'm, uh, usually here on weekends."

"I'll keep that in mind," Candle said, biting in a smile.

"Well, I'll leave you alone then." With obvious reluctance, the young man turned to go just as the waitress reappeared.

Bumping her, his drink spilled, trickling onto Candle's shoulder. "Oh! Hey, I'm sorry!"

"It's okay, really," Candle assured him as she dabbed the spots with her cloth napkin. Then having placed her order for the charbroiled marlin, she excused herself and headed for the women's room.

A bit of water removed the stain, but not the odor, and Candle wondered what Noah would think if she came in smelling like a brewery! She guessed he'd have to think whatever he would because she certainly wasn't explaining. *You're being silly,* she told herself. *He's probably not home anyway.*

Soaping her hands, Candle squinted into the mirror. *Terrible!* she pronounced as she inspected the fresh rash she'd gotten from the heat in Marcy's car. With no makeup on and her hair slicked back, she looked too old, too no-nonsense for Mr. Lifeguard, not to mention too pathetic! And yet the young man had singled her out from the other women alone in the restaurant.

Was she seeing only what she wanted to see, Candle wondered as she headed back to her table. And was Noah?

The young man had left—probably too embarrassed to stay. But her salad waited, and she downed it appreciatively before she remembered that she was in no hurry.

The marlin, a white fillet moist and thick, surpassed her expectations, and Candle savored every bite, prolonging the meal. The texture and taste reminded her more of a center-cut pork chop than fish, and she marveled at the variety of foods and smells and sights from the sea.

The night sky had darkened, but from her window seat, Candle could see the white caps racing to meet one another before casting themselves into foam that washed smooth the sand. A white wing flashed against the navy sea and was gone. She could sit here for weeks.

"Anything else?" the waitress asked, bringing her back to the moment.

Candle shook her head. "Just the bill, please." Paying it, she left reluctantly.

She drove back slowly, then prolonged going in once she'd arrived. Noah had returned before her, just as she'd hoped he would, but now she hoped even more to avoid him. Quietly she slipped in, but Mrs. Cousins caught her.

"The reverend wants to see you in his study."

Candle sighed. "Can't it wait till morning?"

Mrs. Cousins sniffed. "He wouldn't've asked if he hadn't needed something."

"All right, but I'll have to change first. Someone spilled a drink on me."

"H'm. Must've been some party." The housekeeper looked displeased.

Candle smiled. "Actually, a nice but rather careless young man bumped into my waitress. I had dinner alone, Mrs. Cousins. But if you don't mind, I'd like to keep that between you and me."

"No cause to mention it," the housekeeper said, then disappeared into the kitchen.

With a light laugh, Candle started up the stairs just as Noah started down. Her smile vanished, and she froze. Noah stopped too.

"I thought I heard you come in. Did you have a good weekend?"

Sure, Noah. Tasmine and I got along beautifully, and then a young lifeguard toasted me with his drink, she thought. But she said, "It was fine. And yours?"

"Fine."

"Did you want to see me?" *Not that you can't see me. Standing here. Looking awkward.*

57

Noah shook his head. "I found what I was looking for—
that last tape I'd dictated. I had some changes to make."

Candle shifted positions on her corner of the stair.

"I hope you don't mind," Noah added. "The tape—it was
in your room."

"It's your house."

"Candle, while you're here I want you to have privacy. But
I needed that tape, and I didn't know when you'd be back."

"I'm glad you found what you wanted."

Noah looked uncomfortable. "Are you coming up?" he
asked, starting down.

She could turn around. She could go into the kitchen for a
glass of milk. She could pretend she'd left something in the
car. She hesitated only a moment, but by then Noah had
reached her on the stair.

His eyebrow lifted. His lips parted in a soundless question.
His nose twitched, sensing.

Candle stiffened back her shoulders and lifted up her chin.
"Yes, I am going upstairs if you don't mind. I'm tired, and I
need a mouthwash. My breath just *reeks* of marlin!"

chapter
5

IT WAS A STUPID THING TO SAY! Candle chided herself as she got ready for bed. But it was an even more ridiculous situation in which she'd been caught. On the stairs, she'd felt trapped, guilty, defensive. And for what? For taking a day off? For having dinner in a place that served liquor? Every restaurant on the beach served liquor, except the fast-food chains, and she certainly wasn't responsible for that!

Maybe Noah hadn't noticed the smell, she realized rather belatedly, but even if he had, what difference did it make? Her private time was hers to do with as she wished, wasn't it? As long as she did her job, and did it well, he had no cause for complaint.

The problem was, she admitted to herself, that she was doing the very thing she'd vowed *not* to do—getting personally involved. Aside from her capabilities as his hired hands, she could not afford to care about what he thought of her. After all, she'd come to Florida to allow herself some distance from Gary Woodward, and so the last thing she needed was involvement with another employer! Especially one who hid behind a clerical collar!

Somehow she had to get a hold of herself and do the job she'd agreed to do without letting rash judgments or rash words get in the way. *And, Lord, I could use some help with this heat rash too,* she prayed when she'd turned the rest of the problems over to him.

Refreshed, Candle wakened to the sunrise growing golden in the pink sky. Slipping on a robe, she tiptoed onto the balcony, unwilling to disturb the gentle hush that had settled over the beach during the night. No vehicles marred the tide-swept sand, and few feet had left traces, so the world looked newly created and waiting.

It was cooler, Candle realized with a shiver as she stepped inside to dress. Mrs. Cousins had told her the unseasonable heat wouldn't continue, but she'd still parked Marcy's car in the shade, not wanting a repeat of yesterday's oven.

Thinking of her friend, Candle picked up the phone, then set it down again. It was too early to reach Marcy at the office. She'd call her later if Noah didn't have piles of work for her to do in his study.

When she'd washed her face, Candle gave her hair a vigorous brushing before tying it loosely against her neck. The effect softened the harsh lines of the chignon she'd been wearing, making her look closer to her own age rather than to Mrs. Cousins's. She skipped down the stairs to breakfast.

Sitting alone at the kitchen table, Noah seemed surprised to see her.

"You're up early," he commented as he buttered a wedge of whole wheat toast.

"Am I? It's such a lovely morning, it seemed a shame to waste it." She poured herself some juice and sat down.

"Toast?" Noah offered, giving her a curious look.

"Actually I was thinking that an omelet sounded perfect. Want one?"

"Are you making it, or am I?"

"I offered. I'll make it," Candle said, "but you'll have to tell me where Mrs. Cousins keeps things. Where is she, by the way?"

"Taking a walk. We, uh, didn't think you'd be down yet."

Candle decided to ignore the implication. "Really? I didn't see her."

"Oh? Were you out too?"

Candle shook her head as she cracked eggs into a bowl. "Just on the balcony. It's such a magnificent view, I could stay there forever."

Since that was one of those personal comments she'd intended to avoid, she kept silent as she prepared their breakfast. Her feelings, her likes, her dislikes, her needs simply did not fall under the category of business-like conversation.

But Noah did not make her resolution easy. "You enjoy being here, don't you?" he asked, and Candle saw no point in being rude.

"Florida or this house?"

"Both."

"Well, both are lovely. I can't imagine anyone thinking otherwise," she said then bit her tongue. Tasmine had thought otherwise, hadn't she? "Of course," Candle added as she expertly flipped the omelet onto a plate, "I could do without the heat, hives, and antihistamines!"

Noah laughed. "I'm sure you could. Incidentally, your nose is starting to peel." Then to her relief, he turned his attention to the omelet. "Delicious!"

"Thanks, but don't tell Mrs. Cousins," Candle said brightly. "She's such a dear, I wouldn't want her to think she's replaceable."

Over his coffee cup, Noah stared at her thoughtfully. "You're an unusual woman, Miss O'Shea. You know how to laugh. You know how to work. And you care about other people's feelings."

Candle shrugged uncomfortably. "Oh, I don't think that's so unusual," she said, but feeling glad that *he* thought so.

By silent consent, they added dishwashing to the morning's agenda before returning upstairs to a hard day's work. At Noah's request, Candle remained in his study, discussing notes and devising the system she'd proposed for categorizing his research cards. Sometime during the weekend, Noah had purchased a large set of the marker pens she needed, and, business-like, Candle commented on his good memory instead of his thoughtfulness. But secretly, she felt pleased that they made such a nice team.

In the middle of an amicable debate on topic headings, the phone rang, and shortly after, Mrs. Cousins buzzed the study's intercom.

"Sorry to bother you, Reverend, but there's a call for Miss O'Shea from a Marcy John."

Candle groaned at the interruption. "I meant to call her before we began work," she told Noah, and then to Mrs. Cousins, "Tell her I'll phone at lunch."

"She *says* it's urgent," the housekeeper insisted.

Candle sighed. "I'll be right there."

With an apology to Noah, she headed for the sunroom and picked up the receiver. "Marcy, are you all right?"

"Couldn't be better. But I wanted to warn you—Gary will be calling as soon as we free the line."

"Oh." Candle sank onto a corner of her desk. "How did he get this number?"

"From yours truly. I had no choice. He's upset that he hasn't heard from you, and he said he'd come down on the next flight if I didn't tell him where to reach you. I'm sure he meant it."

"Me too. Thanks for the warning." Candle wondered at their choice of the word. Weren't "warnings" reserved for unpleasantries? Yet Gary wanted her to be his wife—a part of himself. Was that so unpleasant?

"Don't hang up!" Candle exclaimed when Marcy started to say goodbye. "I don't have much time now, but I do miss you, and I want to talk to you, yet I don't want to talk, if you know what I mean."

Marcy laughed. "I think so."

"I came by yesterday. You were gone."

"Brad and I went windsurfing. It was great!"

"Oh, I'm so glad!"

They talked a moment longer—each wanting the other's company and yet distracted by the work pressing in for attention. When they hung up, Candle felt relieved they'd been in touch.

The phone rang again, and Candle grabbed the receiver before Mrs. Cousins could pick up the kitchen extension. As expected, Gary's voice shot across the line.

"So, you're alive after all."

"Was there any doubt of that?"

"You don't seem too happy to hear from me." He sounded hurt. "Is something wrong?"

"Just busy."

"Too busy to call or write?"

"Gary, I thought we agreed—"

"What? That you'd take off when you wanted to and go where you wanted to go without a word until you're ready to come back? I don't think you're being fair, Candle."

She supposed he was right. "I'm sorry, Gary. I don't mean to be selfish or difficult, but I do need some time."

"How much time?"

"I don't know! I'll know when I know." And then she added, "A month. Maybe two."

"Two months! Do you need to be away from me that badly?" He sounded hurt again.

"Gary, you know I care about you. But I'm not sure I'm ready to get married."

"Poor Carrot Top. I guess it is a big decision."

She hated it when he called her that. "So you understand?"

"I'm trying. But you could make the waiting easier if you'd pick up the phone once in a while."

"I'll write," she promised. "But, Gary, I can't talk during office hours, so I'd appreciate it if you wouldn't call here again."

"Hey, you're not working for an ogre, are you?"

"No, but I am swamped."

"I wish your friend Marcy would get a phone at that cottage of hers. But, Candle, if I don't hear from you, you know I'll have to call, don't you?"

"I'll write as soon as I can," she said again.

When she'd hung up, she realized she'd done nothing to correct Gary's assumption that she was still staying at Marcy's, and for the first time, she felt grateful that her friend didn't have a home phone. Of course, if Gary knew she not only worked at the Seaton estate but *lived* here, he wouldn't bother to phone. He'd be down on the next flight.

Lord, show me what to do, she prayed.

Noah was waiting, so Candle hurried back to his study, rapping lightly on the door before letting herself in.

"Sorry that took so long," she said, although both phone conversations combined had taken less than ten minutes. "Now, where were we?"

Noah smiled. "Arguing over topic headings."

"Really? I thought we were *discussing* the possibilities."

He laughed. "We were, but your possibilities weren't the same as mine."

Candle gestured in surrender. "You're the boss."

"And you're the one with editorial skills, so you're probably right—about the headings." Noah hesitated. "But some-thing's wrong, isn't it?" He tapped his desk with a pen.

"Everything's fine," Candle insisted. "Or it will be as soon as we get back to work."

For the rest of the day she concentrated reasonably well, giving no thought to Gary's phone call. But Noah himself distracted her more than once. Several times she caught him studying her on the sly, and she didn't know what to make of it. A pastor's concern? An employer's irrational fear that his employee was about to bolt? A man's interest? Candle begged off answering her own questions by throwing herself deeper into work.

What amazed her, however, was that Noah's thesis contin-ued to intrigue her. Although she had written off churchgo-ing, the history of the Christian church fascinated her. Gradually she began to see the church as people—people facing problems, making decisions, and moving forward in their own time, place, and culture until they'd developed a liturgy or worship service right for them. Could there, she wondered, be one right for her?

Leaning over a stack of file cards, Candle tucked away a stray wisp of hair. "Incredible," she said, straightening.

Noah looked up. "What is?"

"The way God took such hopeless, miserable circum-stances—like wars, poverty, persecution, misunderstandings great or small—and turned them into good by using them to spread the church throughout the world. Each denomination that resulted fit the local customs and what the people could or couldn't accept. And yet," she continued, animated, "the basic belief of every parish or congregation is fundamentally the same—Jesus Christ is Lord!"

Nodding, Noah smiled. "That's the unity of the church. For all of its diversity, it's still one family."

"With a touch of sibling rivalry?"

He chuckled. "Well said. But what can you expect from so many personalities?"

Thinking of the church at large as a family unit helped, and even the judgments, backbiting, and pettiness she'd found so offensive, began to make sense. It made her think of the squabbles she and her sister had had as children, each wanting to find special favor in their parents' eyes.

It occurred to her now that Christians wanted to find special favor in the eyes of God. Some tried by religiously following all the rules, some by observing sacraments, some by offering sacrifices. But some, like insecure children, tried to show themselves right by proving others wrong.

Candle shuddered. The last was the church she knew best: a sibling pointing fingers, and often she'd felt mentally and spiritually poked in the eye! That was all she'd known. But if Noah's beliefs and her new thoughts were true, there was more to churchgoing than those negative experiences from childhood.

"Maybe I gave up too soon," she said aloud.

"On the church?"

She nodded. "What I knew was something small, something condemning of me as a person. Yet I felt that God himself was not like that. Oh, I know he has to judge and correct," she hastened to add, "but love—even tough love— is more. I just didn't find that love within the church."

"Yet you still developed a close relationship with God— you said so yourself," Noah reminded her. "I could tell anyway. It's reflected in your eyes, your smile. That's remarkable in a nonchurchgoer!"

Candle laughed. "Spoken like a minister!"

"Probably," he agreed, smiling. "So, indulge my curiosity—how did it happen?"

66

"Through a simple little song," she said, remembering. "When I was, oh, no more than three or four, I attended Sunday school, and my favorite song was 'Jesus Loves Me.' I really *believed* in his love, and it made me love him. As I grew older, however, the church confused me. It presented a God I didn't like because he was so impossible to please! I stopped going to church when my family moved to an area where that denomination didn't exist, and I didn't believe I was missing anything."

"What about your parents? Did they stop going too?" Noah asked.

Candle nodded. "But my dad made up for it by reading the Bible to us regularly. Later I devoured it myself until I was convinced beyond a doubt—Jesus *does* love me. And so does God the Father."

"Go to church with me this Sunday," Noah said suddenly.

"Noah! You didn't hear a word I said."

"But I did. That's why I'm asking. Don't you see? You're *ready* to go back—for your own sake and for mine. You'd be perfect."

She had to smile at his enthusiasm and his choice of words. "Perfect for what?"

"Collaboration. See, it's been my hope all along that this premise—which, as you've noticed, is rather disjointed—will come together when I've *lived* it. I need to be there. I need to *experience* the subtleties, the differences, in each denomination and participate in the worship. Otherwise, anything I have to say will be the mere observation of an outsider."

"I understand. And I agree that your participation will really make this thesis come to life. But surely you can't expect to . . ." She stopped herself from saying "know it all" and added, "to . . . to be in tune with a congregation or parish after only one visit!"

To her dismay, Noah agreed. "That's why I need you along."

She saw his point, and there seemed no gracious way to decline. But Noah didn't leave it there. He made her see that her contribution was truly important to him—another pair of eyes and ears, another watchful spirit. She didn't want to let him down.

"All right! All right! I'll go!" she said, laughing.

But instead of laughing with her, Noah scowled at the calendar in front of him. "I forgot—I promised to serve as chaplain at the local hospital during February. That lets this Sunday out and the next few afterwards. It'll have to be March." He sounded disappointed.

"March is fine. It'll give me time to get used to the idea," she admitted.

"Then it's a date!" Noah said enthusiastically.

A date? She'd hardly call it that. But apparently her racing heart had a vocabulary of its own.

chapter
6

FEBRUARY CAME AND WENT with few changes other than the weather. From her balcony window in the sunroom, Candle watched the early morning shell seekers, wearing scarves or hats and sweaters, and sometimes she went down to join them in their search. Calico scallops, cockles, cones, cerith, and pear whelks soon cluttered a table top, their names combed from a colorful book she'd purchased on Florida shells.

With Noah away at the local hospital on Sundays and Marcy out regularly with Brad, Candle strolled the beach alone as long as she dared. After discovering that her sunscreen lost its effectiveness within two or three hours, she kept a tube in the pocket of her windbreaker, but her nose seemed destined to peel endlessly. She never knew she had so many layers of skin.

As promised, Candle had written Gary every few days, using her "business address" for return. To her relief, he'd answered her letters, not with demanding phone calls, but with brief notes stuffed into Woodward Publishing envelopes, so there'd been no reason for Mrs. Cousins's or Noah's curiosity to be aroused. But the letters were the same—telling her he missed her, asking when she'd come back—and Candle felt so guilty she began to dread their coming. She'd hoped for loving words or chatty news about the office or something to remind her of why she'd been attracted to him in the first place.

Gary is a nice man, she reminded herself—friendly, personable, well liked but firm—a solid core beneath a sensitive exterior. But sometimes she wondered what that core consisted of. Like Marcy, she questioned if the outer man reflected the one inside. Of one thing she was sure, however. She loved her work with Woodward Publishing. Was she, however, confusing this love of a job with affection for the employer? If so, it could happen again.

Realizing this enabled Candle to keep her relationship with Noah in perspective. He needed her help. She needed a salary. And the job proved satisfying to them both. That was enough. And when it was over . . . but, no, she wouldn't let herself think that far.

One day blended into another with the snugness of routine and work well done. Over breakfast, she and Noah would lay out their plans, and for the most part, they'd stick to them, although Candle noticed their schedule was apt to change when they worked together in his study. Then, ideas—and sometimes words—would fly, but even their debates proved fruitful.

When she worked alone, however, Candle knew the day would go as planned. Uninterrupted, she'd transcribe notes before editing the finished copy, then sometime before dinner she'd give the proofed pages to Noah, who, thankfully, was always pleased.

He had an intercom which he seldom used, yet Candle couldn't help but wonder if he didn't purposely avoid coming into her rooms. Perhaps he wanted to prove that he respected her privacy. Or maybe he wanted to avoid reminders of Tasmine.

Candle was surprised, then, the first morning in March, when she heard a tap on the sunroom door. Noah just stood there for a moment, rather shyly, peeking in.

She laughed. "You can come in. I won't throw anything, if that's why you're hesitating."

He stepped in, leaving the door ajar. "Are you in the habit of throwing things?"

"Softballs in grade school. More recently, frisbees, and, of course . . ." She rolled her green eyes. ". . . I've thrown countless wads of paper into the wastebasket."

"I'm afraid you'll have more. No major cause for alarm," he assured her, "but I've discovered one of my secondary sources was too inaccurate for me to use in a thesis. I'll have to scrap the quotes and delete any points gleaned from that text, and that may affect the work we'd outlined for you to do this week."

"Oh, Noah, I'm sorry," Candle empathized. "Look, I'm stopped anyway from doing what we'd planned, so why don't I help you go through the notes and completed pages. We'll be done in no time."

He smiled. "Don't count on it! But, yes, I would appreciate your help."

Noah waited as she gathered the stacks of paper and tapes. It took only a moment to pile the materials, neatly, into a box, and, as she did so, Candle chatted. Noah, however, did not respond.

She looked up and found him staring—not at her, but at the portrait that hung near her desk. Her stomach threatened to capsize under the sudden rush of emotion she felt at seeing Noah's face look so stricken.

Candle glanced away, pretending to be busy, until he asked, "Are you ready?"

"Almost," she answered lightly, handing him the box. "Go ahead. I'll be there in a minute."

As soon as he'd gone, she ran into the bathroom and splashed cold water on her face. Then she grimaced at herself in the mirror. Not a pretty face, compared to Tasmine's. For the first time since her arrival weeks ago, she regretted not having her makeup case along.

"You're being silly," she told her reflection. "You're here to work. Remember?" But it was getting easier to forget. The more she got to know Noah, the more she . . .

Putting the unfinished thought aside, she ran a comb through her hair and retied the low ponytail with a strand of pink yarn.

Lord, help me deal with this, she prayed. Then, standing quietly a moment, the thought came to her, unbidden. *You wonder if Gary is himself, but are you being yourself? Is it fair to you or Noah to be otherwise?*

Squeezing her eyes shut, she sighed deeply. Marcy was right. She wasn't being herself. But who was she anyway? She certainly wasn't glamorous like Tasmine, but neither was she the plain, restrictive person Noah had wanted to hire. Yanking the end of the yarn, she shook her hair free, letting it fall, thick and loose, around her shoulders. Then, with new resolve, she marched into his study.

If Noah noticed anything unusual about Candle's appearance or attitude, he didn't say, and the two worked in silence throughout the morning. The index cards, manuscript pages, and tapes all required editing to delete the problematic reference, and for much of it, Candle had no way of knowing which parts were involved. Since the file cards indicated each resource, she busied herself with pulling the ones that mentioned the particular author and title in question. The work wasn't difficult, just tedious, and it seemed ironic to her that her greatest problem in doing the job was that her hair kept falling in her eyes.

They lunched in the study, scarcely moving or even tasting their food, so intent were they on the project at hand. But when Mrs. Cousins came, mid-afternoon, to pick up their trays, she broke the quietness, scolding.

"It's purely unhealthy the way you two sit there!"

To Candle's surprise, Noah agreed. "As a matter of fact," he said, looking mischievous, "I was thinking a drive down the beach would be nice today—that is, if Miss O'Shea will accompany me."

"Thanks a lot! If I don't go, I'll have your ill health and Mrs. Cousins's wrath on my head!"

Noah grinned. "Does that mean you can't refuse?"

"I wouldn't dare," she said, knowing she wouldn't have anyway.

Lighthearted, she fetched her purse and sweater and joined Noah downstairs, enjoying his well-mannered regard as he opened the car door for her. Courtesy was one of the things she'd appreciated about Gary, but she didn't want to compare. Not right now, anyway.

Inside his silver Mercedes, she buckled up, then settled back comfortably as the car skimmed along the hard-packed sand. Acting as tour guide along a portion of the beach Candle had not yet seen, Noah pointed out the better known resorts and nicer restaurants, but his obvious pleasure came from spotting the fleet appearance of wildlife.

"Porpoises! Did you see them?" He stopped the car, and a dozen sandpipers skittered nervously toward the foamy edge of the sea. "Over there," he exclaimed with delight, pointing until Candle had seen them too.

"Oh, I see! They're playing tag!"

"Looks like it," he agreed as one sleek gray body, then another, cut arcs over the watery horizon.

For a while, they sat with the car windows down, listening

to the thunderous roar of the sea. How restful the sound, how soothing, Candle thought, and how special to be sharing it with Noah.

The salt air tickled her nose, and she inhaled appreciatively. "Delicious!" she said, and he smiled.

Overhead seagulls squawked, amusing her, and Candle commented on the variety in that species. Some were speckled, some black-capped, and some solid white, but all fussed noisily. "I wonder what they're saying?"

Noah chuckled. "They're probably demanding food! They're aggressive birds, but they won't harm you. They're used to being fed by tourists."

"By hand?"

"With snacks and picnic leftovers people have dropped on the beach."

"That's too bad," Candle said, then added lightly, "Maybe that's why they're so fussy! They're telling humans to be less messy."

Noah laughed. Then setting the car in leisurely motion, he pointed out the white tern standing like a statue on the shoreline.

"He's beautiful!" Candle said. "So elegant. So stoic."

"There used to be far more wildlife on the beach than there is now," Noah injected with regret.

"What happened?" she asked, interested.

"Too many cars, I expect. Vehicles aren't allowed around the Cape Canaveral-Cocoa area, and it does make a difference. Come summer time, a sea of cars and trucks are parked three-deep here with two-way traffic besides. The birds and the sea turtles don't have a chance."

"It must be unsafe for children, too." She'd looked toward him as she spoke, and now his eyes caught hers, unsmiling.

"Do you like children?" he asked as though it were terribly important.

"Of course!" she said, then fell with him into a less comfortable silence.

It hadn't occurred to her that he had a destination in mind, but she felt relieved when he steered the car onto a sandy road that connected with the main highway and announced, "Here we are," as they pulled into a small parking lot. A cluster of buildings the color and texture of driftwood apparently housed a group of shops devoted to arts and crafts, and briefly Candle wondered why he'd stopped here.

A sculpted pair of dolphins in one of the charming stores intrigued her. Their poised gracefulness had been so beautifully captured by the artist. "Or are they porpoises?" she asked, uncertain.

"Dolphins," Noah agreed. "They have a blunter nose." And he made a face, mimicking, which Candle found hilarious.

"I like to hear you laugh," he said, a comment that immediately sobered her. Oh, why did he have to make her self-conscious every time she'd begun to relax around him?

Seemingly oblivious to her discomfort, Noah guided her into another, larger room where a wealth of paintings hung, and the touch of his hand on her elbow sent a small electric shock rippling through her arm. She willed herself not to pull away, then concentrated purposefully, slowly, on each painting.

"Oh, isn't that one lovely?" she said, commenting on a huge canvas splashed with exotic fish of varying sizes and colors. "It's so unusual—so full of life."

"It is, isn't it?" Noah agreed. He looked pleased, whether with her comment or her tastes, she didn't know. But before she realized what was happening, he had purchased the painting, had it wrapped, and was wondering if it would fit in the trunk of his car. Fortunately, it did.

He seemed in a hurry on his way home, his thoughts elsewhere, and Candle assumed he was eager to get back to work. But to her surprise when they'd returned, he headed not toward his study but toward her rooms, his unwieldy purchase tucked somehow under his arm.

Bewildered, she asked, "Where . . . What are you doing?"

"Bringing some life back to this house," he answered brusquely.

Candle knew then what the afternoon had been about and wondered if something within her had known all along. There'd been so many beautiful paintings to choose from, but the one that had commanded her attention was exactly the size and subject matter needed to blend with the sitting room's sunny decor. Even the colors were perfect. Still, she looked away as Noah removed Tasmine's portrait, not wanting to see those accusing eyes as he whisked the canvas out of sight.

Tasmine gone! And now, admiring the cheerful new painting, Noah stood looking pleased.

"It's just right, isn't it?"

"Perfect! But, Noah, I . . ."

His hand halted her. "Candle, my marriage was not a successful one, and I don't need reminders of that. The portrait should have come down a long time ago, but until your arrival, I'd pushed it from my mind."

Mutely she nodded. She wanted to thank him, but that seemed inappropriate. Instead she offered, "If you ever want to talk . . ."

"There's not much to say. My wife died in a car accident, and I'd rather not think about the rest. Oh, by the way . . ." he said, patting a bulging pocket on his jacket. "I thought this would be nice on your desk." He pulled out a small package.

"The dolphins!" Candle exclaimed. "Oh, Noah! How thoughtful! They're lovely."

Had he been about to say, "And so are you"? No, her mind was playing tricks, was placing false expectations on what had only been a pleasant, relaxing afternoon—an afternoon that had brought a fresh breath to their work, to this house, this room. Nothing less than that. But nothing more.

"Well!" she said at last, realizing he'd lingered. "Since I have such a delightful work area, I suppose I'd better be getting back to it."

He frowned. "I didn't mean to induce you back to the grindstone." He rubbed his forehead fretfully. "I may be gone a few days." Why did she have the feeling that he'd just come to that conclusion? "Will you have enough to keep you busy with the changes we made today?"

"I don't know."

"Then would you mind working after dinner?"

"Not at all." It was *not* working with him that she minded! She hoped that he'd say something more over dinner about having to be gone, hoped for a clue to his destination or to the purpose of his trip perhaps, but he said nothing, and she didn't want to pry. Well, she did, but she wasn't about to! He'd made it clear from the start that he wasn't interested in any woman who threw herself at him, and since Candle had never witnessed such an occurrence, she had no idea what his interpretation of an aggressive woman was! That he should ever think so of her would be unpardonable—a breach of contract, so to speak.

There was little to say over the meal. Candle emptied her small earthenware bowl of onion soup with no problem, but she toyed with the cherry tomatoes on her salad, wondering when alfalfa sprouts, lettuce, and avocado had become such burdens to chew.

Noah seemed to be having the same difficulty. "Would you like some music?" he asked while they waited for the main course of the meal.

"Yes. Please."

He didn't ask her preference but put on a tape of soothing yet somewhat eerie strains Candle had never heard before.

"H'm. Nice. Who's the composer."

For the first time since the awkward hanging of the new painting, Noah smiled. "I thought I'd catch you on that one. The composer is a young man who calls himself John Doe."

Candle's laughter spilled across the marble table. "Ah, Mr. Doe! Now don't tell me," she insisted playfully. "Let me guess. With a name like that, this must be a contemporary piece, right?"

Noah nodded.

"I know!" She leaned back as Mrs. Cousins set a platter of lemon buttered grouper on the table. "It's the sound track from a science fiction movie."

Noah beamed. "Right. How'd you guess?"

Candle helped herself to a dollop of sour cream on her baked potato. "That unearthly quality gives it away," she admitted. "Besides, most of the brilliant music being written today is motion picture scores."

"And I thought you were brilliant to guess," he teased.

She wished he wouldn't make that kind of comment. "But I never, ever would've guessed the composer was John Doe," she said, and their laughter recaptured the light moment.

With restful, more familiar music playing, they finished Mrs. Cousins's delicious dinner. Then they took their after-dinner coffee upstairs and worked far later than either had intended.

With enough to keep her occupied for several days, Candle scanned the files they'd reorganized, satisfied that the work could progress smoothly in Noah's absence. He'd merely told her he'd be near a place called Siloam Springs and that Mrs. Cousins could reach him in an emergency. He had apologized to Candle for the delay in their church outings, but she had felt relieved. Attending church, even with Noah, was not high on her list of things to do.

"Noah," she said now as she reread the introduction he'd completed. "What will happen to this thesis after you've received your doctorate?"

With a shrug, he looked up from the desk he'd been straightening. "I hope it'll be published in a theological journal. Why?"

"Just wondering. It seems a shame for all of this research and effort and ideas to . . . to . . ."

". . . gather dust on a *dry* shelf," he finished for her.

"H'm." She hadn't meant to offend him, but that was exactly what she was going to say. Fortunately Noah didn't seem the least perturbed.

Candle, however, felt regretful that Noah's work wouldn't reach the general public, and she couldn't leave the idea alone. What would it take, she wondered, to make the paper more readable, more conversational? Snatching up the outline, she studied it carefully. It would take time, but she could delete most of one section, expand the others, rework the overall tone, and . . . yes! She could do it!

"You're looking pleased," Noah said, startling her. How long had he been watching?

"For your information, I am!" she said smugly, not bothering to deny it. Quickly she told him what she'd been thinking. "I don't know too much about the ecumenical movement," she admitted, "except that there is one—but doesn't that make this work timely? And don't people need to know?"

Looking amused, Noah agreed. "But, Candle, aren't you forgetting something? I'm not a writer of popular prose nor an editor! So I'm not at all sure I could do the kind of book that people would buy."

"I can," she said with such confidence, he smiled.

"Does that mean you're hiring yourself for the job?"

"Only if you promise to collaborate."

He leaned back in the leather chair. "Shouldn't we negotiate first? Salary or royalty split?"

"Royalties—fifty-fifty."

He laughed. "You *are* confident this book will sell!"

She made a face. "Of course."

"Will you work here?"

The confidence faded, and she faltered. She couldn't work at Marcy's with no income for sharing expenses. But neither could she enjoy the luxurious room and board at Noah's without an invitation. She'd have to get another job, and then she wouldn't have much time to devote to working on a publishable manuscript.

"It'd be difficult to, uh, collaborate if you weren't here," Noah said.

"And my friend, Marcy, doesn't have a phone."

He thumped the desk. "Then it's settled. You'll stay."

"But what about Mrs. Cousins?" Hesitantly, she pointed out, "My being here creates extra work for her, Noah, and she fusses when I try to help. She won't even let me do my own laundry! I'm sure she's well paid, but not to baby-sit me!"

He smiled. "Don't worry about Mrs. Cousins, Candle. She's happiest when she has someone to fuss over, and I'm not usually here every day. Besides," he added with amusement lightening his dark eyes, "she likes having you around. And so do I."

"Oh." She didn't know what else to say.

Her hand fluttered against her neck, like a moth seeking warmth, but Noah arose from his desk, extending his own hand toward her.

"Partners," he said with a firm shake to seal their agreement.

"Partners," she replied as their fingers clasped tightly.

The impact of his touch almost staggered her, and quickly she sat down. Noah did likewise—immediately busying himself with a stack of papers he'd already straightened. Could their touch have jolted him too?

Candle doubted it, but at least he'd said he liked having her around—which probably meant he didn't find her annoying! Well, that was important, she realized—especially if they'd be working together for months to come.

Months! *Gary!* Suddenly Candle wondered what she'd gotten herself into. Gary would not sit idly by, waiting patiently for her to finish a book co-authored by another man! Unless, she thought, she could interest him in the project. Slim chance, she realized, and yet Woodward Publishing was the company she knew best. It was worth a try—if she could just figure how to go about it.

Looking up, Noah caught her staring. "Already imagining my photo on a book jacket?" he asked lightly.

"A turtleneck sweater, a tweed jacket, and, of course, a pipe," she answered in kind.

He grinned. "Spoken like a true editor-author. But do you think my alleged audience would object to a clerical collar?"

She'd never seen him in one, and trying to picture it now, the image made her sad. Without answering, she squinted at him, thinking.

"Or maybe the collar would make me look stuffy. I'm not, you know." But his voice sounded starched.

It didn't help that he'd expressed what she'd felt—the remoteness that she'd feared and chosen to ignore. His clerical collar was a fact—a reality—but, she told herself, it was only a piece of cloth, a prop, a symbol. Yet it represented his profession, which was not writer, but pastor-priest, and, whether she liked it or not, his church stood between them, more threatening than any other human, any other woman, any other love could be.

chapter
7

BEFORE NOAH'S DEPARTURE, Candle sought his advice about a reputable garage, one preferably close by so she wouldn't have to wait around for a tune-up. But Noah wouldn't hear of her walking in the Florida sun.

"What are you doing with that piece of junk anyway?" he'd asked on the way back from the garage. "Doesn't Woodward Publishing pay you enough to buy a decent car?"

"Yes, but I, uh . . ." she hesitated, feeling foolish. "It's Marcy's car. I borrowed it," she admitted, not wanting to reveal that Marcy had hers.

Since she had so seldom driven anywhere the last couple of months, she hadn't given the car exchange much thought. But now she wished she hadn't switched automobiles in the first place. It'd be hard to explain—if, of course, she ever had to—and Candle didn't know if Noah would see the humor in the situation.

Having him away was no fun either, particularly when she didn't know how long he'd be gone. Yet the hours flew as she poured herself into the editing and typing of his manuscript.

Although she delayed mentioning the book in her letters to Gary, Candle itched to get on with it. She felt certain it'd be useful and well received. That wasn't the job she'd been hired to do, she realized, but she discovered that ideas for the book came to her as she worked on Noah's doctoral thesis.

Her interest in the text amazed her, and she attributed that to Noah's style. His wit enlivened the scholarly tone, and his generous use of illustrations kept the work from becoming boring. Nevertheless, his subject matter remained solidly the church.

Candle sighed. The judgmental attitudes in her childhood church had made her judgmental toward the whole body of Christ! Wanting to change that thinking, she had agreed to attend services with Noah. Meanwhile, his love of the church made her feel . . . how? She wasn't sure.

What is it, Lord? she decided to ask, and Noah's words came immediately to her mind.

"I need to be there," he'd said. "Otherwise, anything I have to say will be the observations of an outsider."

An outsider, Candle mused. Yes, that was how she felt.

Wistfully she stroked the pewter-colored backs of the sculpted dolphins Noah had bought for her. She needed no reminder of their time together, but the beautiful memory made the artistry seem fitting—a pair. No outsiders to intrude. A work, a memory, completed.

Reluctantly, Candle pulled her hand away from the dolphins and set her fingers in motion on the heavy-duty typewriter Noah had provided. When she had to retype a page, she wished again for a word processor, especially since she now had a full book to do. But she was reluctant to ask Noah again.

All in all the work went well, and Candle hoped Noah would be pleased. She herself felt satisfied, often working into the night until Mrs. Cousins reminded her, "A body needs food, rest, and fresh air!"

Heeding the housekeeper's sensible advice, Candle treated

herself to solitary walks on the beach after the sun had sunk low on the horizon. But the quietude she'd come to expect was broken by the influx of college students, who crowded the beach now that spring break was here. They were so rowdy and silly that she could hear them from the pool. Occasionally she took a dip, swimming ten laps or more to exercise her stiff neck and shoulder muscles. But mostly she spent her spare moments editing and revising the manuscript she'd begun from Noah's outline and notes.

Ironically, however, the book forced her thoughts toward Gary, and Candle knew she couldn't put him off much longer. She'd come to Florida to allow herself some distance, some time to think, but she'd wound up thinking about him rarely, if at all. Even now, he came into mind only because of Noah. She could, she supposed, contact another publisher about the book, but Woodward Publishing had been "home" for a long time, and Candle felt her experience there might give the manuscript some advantage. Besides—she had to tell Gary about it sooner or later.

She decided to make it later. Instead she gave her parents a call to check on them and let them know how she was doing. The she phoned Marcy.

"Candle!" her friend exclaimed. "Long time no see."

She laughed. "I couldn't have said it better."

"Well, you know how it is with us advertising people— we're full of fresh, catchy phrases. So, how've you been?"

"Good," Candle responded. "Busy."

"If I know you, that means good and busy," Marcy scolded. "Any chance I can drag you away from your tall, dark, handsome, and strange employer?"

"Delete the 'strange,'" Candle stated firmly. "But if you want to get together, I'd love to."

"Aha! Bet he's not there."

"Marcy!"

"Okay, I get the message. You don't want to discuss him. See you Saturday for brunch? My place?"

"I'll be there," Candle promised.

As soon as she'd hung up, she regretted the commitment. Although she certainly wanted to see Marcy, she didn't want to miss Noah. There was so much to tell him . . . So many ideas to flesh out . . . So . . .

Who are you kidding? she asked herself. *Admit it! You just want to see him. To show him how very efficient you've been while he was away?* No, she didn't think so.

When the second Saturday in March arrived—and Noah didn't—Candle set off for the beach cottage. In the sandy driveway, she tapped the horn, announcing her arrival, and Marcy ran out to greet her.

Standing back on the weathered porch, they exclaimed over one another as though years had gone by instead of weeks.

"Your skin looks terrific! You look terrific! My car looks terrific! What did you do to it anyway?" Marcy pointed toward her old clunker.

"It needed a tune-up, so I asked the garage to have someone throw on a wax job. The guy said it was probably a first!" Candle teased.

"Not true! I waxed that car myself once, oh, about three years ago," Marcy protested, laughing. "Come sit down and tell me what you've been up to," she said, sinking into the porch rocker.

Candle settled onto the vinyl cushion of a natural wicker settee. "So much has happened, I hardly know where to start."

"Then tell me if you've gotten yourself into anything you wished you hadn't," Marcy coaxed.

That seemed easy enough. "Well, I did agree to do something I never intended to do."

Marcy rocked forward. "What! What? Tell me! This sounds scandalous!"

Candle laughed. "I promised to visit different church denominations with Noah."

Marcy threw a hand across her forehead. "Shocking! Why would you agree to do such a thing?"

"To help him with his thesis . . . Now, Marcy, stop it! I'm serious! You know how I am about church."

"Yeah." Her friend patted her arm. "Hey! Would it help if Brad and I come with you? Or, rather, you two come with us."

"H'm. I hadn't thought of that. When?"

"Tomorrow. Next Sunday. Whenever. You name it."

Candle cocked her head. "So, you and Brad have a standing date for church services?"

Marcy shrugged. "Sort of."

"This is sounding serious! You two must've really hit it off!"

Marcy grinned broadly. "What can I say? The man thinks I'm clever, witty, gorgeous, and a gourmet cook. Who am I to knock his tastes?"

Candle laughed. "He's right on all counts."

The curly head shook a cheerful denial. "No, but maybe the potential is there, and I'll evolve. Anyway, I always did like a man who sees the best in me, don't you? Candle? Why are you looking at me funny?"

"Am I? Just thinking. Your relationship with Brad sounds long term, and I'm so glad!" She lifted an eyebrow. "Marcy! I've never seen you blush before! You really are serious about him.

"I'm sitting in the sun!" She hopped up from the rocker, her cheeks even pinker now. "What am I thinking about— keeping you outside!"

Although she'd been completely in the shade, Candle followed her friend into the cottage's pleasant interior. If Marcy wanted to talk about Brad, they'd talk. But Candle mentally vowed not to press her. She didn't feel ready to share her own feelings about Noah, and she supposed that new relationships were too delicately woven to bear too much handling in conversation—even between closest friends.

"Oh, by the way," Marcy called over her shoulder as Candle shut the front door. "Am I to take it that congratulations are in order for you and Gary?"

"What do you mean?"

"That you and Gary are *not* going to make the mistake of marrying each other," Marcy said as she pulled a bowl out of a lower cabinet.

"H'm," Candle said noncommittally as she excused herself to freshen up.

It disturbed her that her friend reacted so strongly to Gary, and she wondered how Marcy would respond to Noah. Even more, she wondered how Noah would respond to her if she enhanced her looks instead of downplaying them.

"Don't let me forget my makeup case," she called to Marcy, who was busily preparing something in the kitchen.

"It's by the sofa," her friend hollered back. "I thought you might be needing it, so I set it out."

"Marcy!" It was Candle's turn to blush. "See, Brad was right. You *are* clever."

The mop of curls bounced into the living room. "Intuitive maybe, but not clever. The Barnaby account I was working on fell through, and Seaton Industries gave me a 'Don't call us, we'll call you.'"

"Oh, Marcy, I am sorry," Candle exclaimed. She knew how hard her friend had worked, and she wished she could help alleviate the disappointment. "It takes time to build a reputation for excellence. But you'll do it, Marcy! I just know you will." She chewed her lower lip thoughtfully, hesitantly, wondering if it would do any good for her to speak to Noah about the Seaton account.

When she looked up, Marcy was shaking her head at her. "No, I don't want you to talk to your reverend. I'll just have to stretch until I can reach what I want."

"You've been doing that—and very well," Candle reminded her. Your own office, a part-time receptionist—all in the last few months! But you're so clever you probably knew I had no doubts."

"Intuitive," Marcy corrected.

"Then put that trait to work for you in finding out what people need before they're even aware of it!"

"H'm. A clever deduction," Marcy said, and they both giggled.

The smell of lobster quiche coaxed them back into the kitchen, and they chatted about their jobs as they finished preparing brunch. Marcy rushed about, filling the teapot and checking the slowly browning crust, while Candle set out silverware and folded colorful cloth napkins. By the time the quiche had cooled properly, Candle had described Noah's current project and sketched out her ideas for his book.

"Now *that's* clever." Marcy poured their tea.

"What?"

"You've only been on the job a couple of months, and you've already managed to extend it! Surely your reverend wouldn't hire someone else for a job you've created."

Candle laughed. "I hope not! I like working for Noah— especially since I no longer have a portrait of his wife staring over my shoulder."

"Tasmine?"

"How did you know her name?"

89

Marcy looked sheepish. "I asked a guy I know who works at Seaton Industries."

"Marcy!"

"Listen, kid, that's what friends are for. There you were rushing off to some strange man's estate—yes, I asked about that too. And you acted as though you'd been hypnotized. Since I'd been procrastinating on seeking Seaton Industries' account anyway, I decided it was time to do a little, uh, research for both of us."

"And you approached them before you were ready." Candle paused with the realization. "Oh, Marcy, you *are* a friend! And such a dear one. But surely you didn't think I'd get involved beyond what I could handle?"

"You tell me," Marcy said. Candle knew she meant Gary. But the two men were so very different, the situation so different. Or was it?

Candle sighed. "I'm not sure I want to know what you found out."

"You do," Marcy assured her. "But it can wait while we relax over lunch. I want this quiche to be appreciated, and it's getting cold!"

"Spoken like a true gourmet," Candle teased, and they both laughed.

They ate quietly, talking of neutral matters until the ironstone plates had been rinsed for the dishwasher. Then taking their refilled cups into the living room, they each curled up in a corner of Marcy's overstuffed sofa.

"Okay. Tell me," Candle said, breaking the silence.

Marcy sipped her tea slowly. "Tasmine," she said at last, "was a knockout—the kind of beauty that turns heads, male and female."

Candle nodded. "I could see that from her portrait."

"Noah was absolutely smitten with her—too much so,

probably, to be aware of the person he'd married. But, in the beginning, he adored her."

Could he be afraid now of any attractive woman? Candle suddenly wondered. *Afraid?* No, that wasn't it. Cautious, certainly, but what?

"Of course, Noah didn't stay mesmerized," Marcy continued. "Tasmine was neither goddess nor saint. Whether or not she loved him or just his money, I don't know, because there are differing opinions on that. Incidentally, I was discreet in asking questions."

"I'm sure you were."

"Anyway, Tasmine had an enormous need for attention that one man couldn't possibly fill." Marcy paused again, letting her words sink in, and when they did, Candle suddenly envisioned the lovely cream and white bedroom—so elegant, so refined, so *chaste*. No wonder Tasmine hated it!

"Noah was devastated when he learned about his wife's, uh, escapades," Marcy went on. "Understandably, he brought up the topic of divorce, but she responded with some very nasty scenes."

"Wait a minute!" Candle held up her hand. "That's just gossip."

Marcy shook her head. "At least some of her scenes were staged during working hours at Seaton Industries. As I said, Tasmine craved attention. Lots of it."

Candle shuddered. No wonder Noah didn't want to talk about it! Oh, he must have been furious! Was that it? Was he still angry?

"How sad for both of them," Candle said half to herself, half aloud.

Marcy nodded. "But it was the very awfulness of the situation that apparently brought Noah to his knees."

"But isn't that sad too? Or at least ironic? Tasmine drove

him to his search for God, and then she lost him completely in his church!" Candle sighed. "I wonder if any woman could accept having her husband's commitment divided between marriage and the church?"

Marcy laughed. "You're asking *me*?"

Candle frowned. "What? Oh. I forgot. You're Roman Catholic. Well, there is something to be said for the celibate life, isn't there? I'd just never thought about it before." Noah's church didn't require such vows, but Candle wondered how well he could handle the balance between church and home. He seemed so devoted, so married, to his work.

"Want me to go on?" Marcy asked. "About the accident, I mean."

"Please," Candle said. It'd done no good to ignore Tasmine's existence in Noah's life. Perhaps if she had more light, she could understand the present in terms of the past. Or was it the future that really concerned her?

"When Noah left the business world for seminary," Marcy continued, "Tasmine became more open about her partying. She began drinking—heavily. She collected speeding tickets like trading stamps and eventually lost her license and her looks." Marcy hesitated then finished in a rush. "She was drunk. She was driving. She crashed her Porsche, head-on, against a pier."

Candle gasped and covered her eyes to block out the sight. "No one else was hurt?"

"There was a man in the car with her, and he, too, was killed instantly," Marcy added regretfully. "It's only gossip, of course, but he was rumored to have been more than a friend."

And Noah? Candle thought as the last piece slipped into place. *Noah never forgave her. And probably never forgave himself.*

92

chapter
8

NOAH'S DISTRUST—HIS DISLIKE—OF ATTRACTIVE WOMEN was rooted in an unforgiving attitude, Candle realized with a shock. She'd thought him biased, even sexist, and she'd assumed he had his reasons, but unwillingness to forgive was not one she had considered.

She tried to hear what Marcy was saying after that, but concentrating on other lighter topics was too much of a strain, and finally she gave up the effort. With makeup case in tow, Candle rushed through their goodbyes somewhat earlier than she'd expected, wanting to be alone.

"Don't forget!" Marcy called after her as she hurried toward her car.

"What?"

"Brad and I will be at eleven o'clock mass if you and Noah want to make it a foursome."

"Oh, yes—thanks. If he's home by then . . ."

Candle liked the thought of having Marcy along, and so she promised to ask Noah. She felt certain he'd consent gladly—especially since his research had begun, historically, in chronological order. St. Michael's seemed the obvious place to begin.

"Look for us—this Sunday or next."

"I'll give you a call," Marcy promised.

Inside the snug familiarity of her sports car, Candle's thoughts returned to Noah. *Unwillingness to forgive!* It amazed and saddened her. Had she thought he'd be exempt?

As she drove down the beach, her car weaving in and out of the throngs of sun seekers, she noticed a small vehicle parked on the edge of the shore. Apparently the owner had ignored the signs that warned against parking on the water side of the beach, and as long as he didn't get a ticket, he'd have no cause for concern. It was low tide. But he'd have a problem if he were still there when the tide came in.

When she was out of sight of the cottage, she parked on the hard-packed sand, carefully avoiding the deeper drifts. To get stuck in loose, dry sand was easy to do. Dry sand. Loose sand. Or the wet, sucking sand of high tide. Getting caught took no effort, but getting free was usually impossible without help.

Was that what had happened to Noah? Was he stuck in an unforgiving attitude? She ached for him—and for Tasmine too—for the pain they'd caused one another, the agony they'd endured, and the awfulness that touched Noah even now.

Set the wheels straight. Rock the car. Reverse the gears— backwards, forwards.

She got out of her car and sat in its shade for a long time, praying, wondering when the tide would change. *Oh, Lord, is there nothing I can do?* she cried out.

The ocean waves were soothing, calming. Candle breathed in the salt-sprayed air and listened to the pounding surf pulsating with regularity. Nothing, nothing, nothing she could do, but pray. And yet—wasn't that everything?

Of course, she thought, but surely Noah had prayed! Surely he—a man of God—had asked the Lord to heal him. Unless

. . . unless he'd drifted into it without knowing . . . unless he was unaware that he was stuck . . . unless he couldn't dig out without someone else's help. He was, after all, human.

And so was Tasmine. Not a goddess to be adored, but a person hungry for love.

Oh, Lord God, help Noah to forgive her! Candle prayed now. *Help him to forgive himself in Jesus' name.*

She sat, then, peacefully looking out at the sea, lost in its timelessness, and knowing that God the Creator of time and space could reach back into the past and bring forth healing.

The glistening white sail of a catamaran caught her eye and brought her back into the present. She noticed that the tide was coming in, skirting the beach road with foamy ruffles. Time to leave. Time to let go of the moment.

Not wanting to get stuck on the beach, which was now more putty than road, Candle exited her car onto a soft side road that connected with the main highway. Her wheels spun in the light drift, gained traction, then jerked onto pavement, and she sighed her relief.

When she reached the Seaton estate, marveling again at its size and beauty, she spotted Noah's car in the driveway. Good. He was back.

She looked down to the beach. There he was—surfing in his wetsuit. She wished she could run down to the water and tell him that everything would be all right—the Lord promised healing. But instead she walked down slowly, not wanting to interrupt his rare time of relaxation, not wanting to interfere with a process between him and God. She'd done what she could to bathe the past in prayer, but the real cleansing was up to the Lord.

Skimming across an ocean swell on his surfboard, Noah looked remarkably agile and young. His trim, muscled body swayed in well-controlled movements designed to make the most of the wave and to keep afloat. A surge of whitewater curled suddenly around him, and he crashed into the foam. When he came up out of the water, he shook his dark, dripping head like a wet puppy. Then, straddling his board, he paddled out again with his hands.

After watching a few runs, Candle stopped holding her breath and decided that surfing looked like fun. Maybe Noah would teach her. He obviously knew what he was doing, although she had to wonder if the short sleeves on his wetsuit were adequate in the cool water.

He still had not seen her. When he did, he waved, then tucked his board under his arm and came up out of the water. She'd thought he would do that, and since he did, she was doubly glad that she'd obeyed her inclination to leave him alone.

She wondered now if he'd be as happy to see her as she was him. But as he neared the spot where she'd been standing quietly, she could see a scowl cross his face. What had she done wrong? Had he checked her work, disapproving of it, while she'd been out? Was he irritated that she'd taken time off? What?

He charged toward her rapidly, waving his free arm in the direction of the driveway, and as soon as he was within earshot over the ocean's roar, he shouted, "Where did you get that?"

Puzzled, Candle stared at him a moment before following his finger's direction. Her car! Her red sports car! How on earth did it get here? She'd driven it, of course—had even sat near it all afternoon without once realizing she'd left Marcy's old clunker behind! Oh, she hoped Marcy had an extra set of keys.

"The car," Noah repeated. "Where did it come from?"

"It's . . . It's mine," Candle stammered. "I'd loaned it to Marcy. Remember? I borrowed hers. Does . . . Does it matter?"

Noah sank onto a wrought iron settee and dropped his forehead into his wet hands. "No. It doesn't matter. It just gave me a start, seeing it in the driveway." His low voice trailed off, and Candle could see he was shaken.

Tasmine's sports car! Yes, the lines of Candle's far less expensive make were similar from the side, and undoubtedly the Porsche was also red.

"Noah, I'm sorry. Really. I never meant to stir up bad memories for you."

"Memories?" Noah's glazed eyes cleared. "I hadn't realized . . . But, yes, you're right." He was speaking to himself, not her, and Candle suspected that she was witnessing the beginning of healing.

"Would you like for me to swap back with Marcy?" she asked, but Noah shook his head.

"The past is past, and I'd rather leave it alone. Besides, I'm glad you have a decent car." He squinted at the sky. "Want to go for a walk? Or is there still too much sun for you?"

She smiled. "I'm taking your doctor friend's advice and using a sunscreen whenever I'm out. A walk would be . . . nice." She had wanted to say, ". . . a wonderful way to celebrate," but he wouldn't know what she was talking about. For now, it was enough that his thoughts had turned so quickly from past to present, with concern for her. It was enough that he wanted to go for a walk—together.

In amiable silence, they strolled down the beach, and when Noah's hand reached out for hers, that too felt comfortable. Candle had taken off her sandals, and they swung now from the crook of her fingers as she padded across the putty-like sand. Around her feet, the foamy edge of the sea licked her toes, and deposited seaweed like so many tangles of water-dulled beads.

Gifts—all of it! Dreamily, she gazed out over the horizon at the thin line that divided the deeps—water and sky—and it was good.

A fresh wash of sea bubbles tickled her bare feet, and Candle gave a little shriek. Then, laughing, she broke into a run, splashing along the water's edge. Noah followed in her wake, and the chase was on, leaving Candle feeling exhilarated. Wasn't that what she'd wanted ever since she'd met him? For *Noah* to chase *her*.

Without giving him a warning, she abruptly slowed her pace, and Noah fell against her, catching himself and her in a whirl until they'd both regained their balance.

Playfully he squeezed her. "I needed that!" he said, less breathless than she, and Candle knew he meant the fun, not the exercise.

She tried to say, "Me too," lightly, but her lips parted, and no words came.

His bright smile vanished as he searched her face, his dark eyes like moonlight playing on the water. Candle held her breath. His strong arms tightened around her. "You're trembling," he said. "Cold?"

She shook her head.

Lifting her chin, his eyes traced her forehead, her hair, her nose, her lips, and for a moment, she thought he meant to kiss her. "I missed you," he said, as though just realizing it himself.

She smiled. "Because I'm indispensable?"

He frowned. "No, because I . . ." He stopped himself, leaving her to fill in the blank. "I needed to get away, but it's good to be home," he finished simply, his arms dropping to his sides. "Ready to walk back?"

She nodded, feeling a stab of disappointment. What had he started to say? And why hadn't she told him she had missed him too? The silence suddenly seemed unbearable, and Candle began to chat as they strolled leisurely toward the house, catching him up on the work she'd done and the progress made on the book. As she'd hoped, her small talk and enthusiasm lightened the mood. "I can hardly wait to get your feedback."

"Not tomorrow though. It's Sunday," he reminded. "Do you still plan to attend church with me?"

"Of course! I said I would."

"I know, but I may have pushed too hard. I'd rather you go because you want to."

"I do," she said truthfully, even though she didn't particularly look forward to the event.

"Good!" he exclaimed, relieved. "Any place in particular you'd prefer?"

Candle was pleased he'd given her a choice. "I'd like to start with St. Michael's, if you don't mind. Chronologically, it seems like the place to begin, and my friend Marcy John attends there. She and her friend Brad are planning on the eleven o'clock service."

"Then eleven o'clock it is," Noah said amiably. "And I'm glad you'll be well fortified with friends."

As they neared his house, Noah gave a wave to an older woman coming toward them, calling out, "Irene!" Then to Candle he explained, "She's a member of my church."

With so many swimmers, joggers, and strollers on the beach, Candle supposed it was to be expected that Noah would be acquainted with some, but she regretted the loss of privacy. For a short while, he'd been hers. They'd been a pair. No outsiders.

"Oh, Noah, dear, how delightful to see you!" Irene called

as she neared them. "I was hoping I might catch you outdoors on this delectable spring day! And, my! What a lovely companion you have." The older woman extended her hand, and Candle clasped it warmly. "You look familiar to me, dear. Have we met?"

"I've seen you on the beach, shelling, but we've never introduced ourselves. I'm Candle O'Shea—Noah's secretary."

"Don't let her fool you, Irene. She's more than that!" he said as Candle's heart soared. "She's my manuscript assistant, editor, typist, and soon-to-be co-author."

"And a charming companion," Irene finished with an impish grin.

"That too," Noah agreed.

The wrinkled face sought his lovingly. "I don't mean to embarrass you, dear, but playing becomes you." Then turning to Candle, she added, "He works entirely too hard, and if I were, oh, thirty years younger, I'd put a stop to that. I'd make him have a good time whether he wanted to or not."

Candle laughed. "I'm sure you could. And I do agree, Irene. He works too hard."

"Not that you do," Noah injected under his breath.

"Did you know," Irene went on, "that our young reverend here has rebuilt an ailing church to over a thousand active members!"

"Very interesting," Candle said, giving Noah a sharp look. "No, he's never told me about his accomplishments. A thousand members, huh?" She made a face as Noah shrugged off the accolade.

"But my dear!" Irene exclaimed. "That's not the half of it! He knows everyone by name! Can you imagine what a joy that is for those of us who are alone? Except for this young man's attention, we rarely hear our names spoken. We're seldom touched or held. But when Noah's at church, we know we're in for a bear hug!" She held out her hand to him. "Oh, my! I have surely missed you, Rev. Seaton."

Candle bit her lip and widened her eyes to keep from crying as Noah gave the older woman a hug. How healing his touch must be—and to so many! A thousand people! Candle had had no idea.

Suddenly she remembered the scene with Mrs. Powers at the employment agency. No wonder Noah had been annoyed when she didn't remember his name! To remember a thousand names . . . she wondered how he did it, and then she simply supposed it was because he cared.

A calico scallop, shaped and ribbed like an open fan, caught Irene's attention, and she hurried toward it, outracing the sweep of the tide. Then, scooping up the golden brown shell, she rinsed it in sea water before stuffing in into her pocket.

Candle watched as another treasure enticed her further down the shore. "What a delightful woman, Noah! I hope the other *nine hundred and ninety-nine* people in your church are half as dear."

He grimaced. "I wish," he said, ignoring her emphasis on the size of his flock.

Suddenly it seemed important to ask, "Is Irene widowed?"

Noah nodded. "Charles died less than two years ago."

"Were they married a long time?" Candle had to know.

"Over forty years."

"I can see why. Irene is a beautiful woman—inside and out." Watching his face, Candle squinted up at him and added, "I bet she was a real knockout when she was young."

Raised eyebrows indicated his surprise, but Noah didn't say a word. As Irene came toward them again, however, holding out her newest find, Candle caught him watching the older woman with a speculative look. *Thanks, Lord, for that word,* she thought, feeling pleased.

"Candle, look! See what I've found!" Irene called. Excitedly she waved a dull gray shell, flat and round. "A sand dollar! And not a chip missing!" Carefully, she placed the shell in Candle's hand.

"That is a find!" Candle fingered the treasure, noting it felt like a round of unglazed clay. On the top side, small vents sliced through the delicate floral pattern.

"Keep it, dear. It's yours."

"Oh, I couldn't, Irene," she started to protest.

"But I insist! I have a dozen more at home, but this one's special, dear. To find unbroken sand dollars," she went on, explaining, "I look early in the morning when few people are stirring. But this one has come at the end of a day with youngsters and cars swarming about, and so, you see, dear, it's an unexpected treasure—something special."

Candle didn't know what to say as she gave the older woman a hug.

Nor were there words to meet the softness in Noah's eyes as he stood quietly watching. "Well, ladies, if you'll excuse me. I'm going to go peel out of this wetsuit. It's warm, and I feel like a rubber duck out of water."

Irene giggled. "Don't let me stop you, dear." She returned his kiss on the cheek. "Oh, Noah!" Immediately she called him back. "I almost forgot . . . Someone at Trinity keeps asking if I've seen you, and she's so difficult to avoid . . ." Her voice trailed off.

"Who is it?" Noah asked.

Irene gave Candle an apologetic look. "Rebecca Townsend. She's been quite displeased by your absence, so I'm rather surprised she hasn't descended upon you here. She really can make a nuisance of herself, though it seems unkind to say so!" Looking dismayed, the older woman pressed her hand against her mouth.

"I appreciate your telling me," Noah consoled, "but don't worry about Becky." Then brushing the remark aside, he waved goodbye and headed for the house.

Candle watched him go. His response had seemed casual enough, yet she'd sensed his tension at the mention of Rebecca Townsend's name. Or was the agitation her own, Candle wondered, as she watched the Rev. Seaton of Trinity Church disappear from sight.

chapter
9

As PROMISED, Marcy called the next morning, and Candle arranged to meet her and Brad in the churchyard at St. Michael's. Then, remembering that her friend didn't have a phone, she asked, "Where are you now?"

"At Brad's. He promised to make breakfast if I'd squeeze the oranges, but he failed to tell me he doesn't have an automatic juicer. Good thing I arrived early. I'd offer to pick you two up," Marcy went on, "but my old car makes a lousy limousine."

"Oh, Marcy! I hope you had an extra set of keys! I don't know what's gotten into me lately."

"I do." Marcy chuckled.

To run off, unthinking, in her own car, yet remembering to take her makeup case and a few choice outfits was rather telling, Candle supposed, as she hung up the phone. Except for lip gloss, she decided to skip the makeup, but took out one dress then another before choosing a long-sleeved, loose-fitting shirtwaist of pink silk.

Noah admired her selection. "I thought redheads couldn't wear pink."

"That's a myth," Candle said, as he guided her out the door and toward his car. "Probably started by a raven-haired beauty who wanted to keep the color to herself."

A cool breeze played across the ocean water, and Candle was glad she'd brought a lightweight shawl. Marcy had assured her that a head covering was no longer required for women entering the church, so Candle slid the shawl beneath her thick tresses. For such a warm winter, this almost spring weather felt cool.

"Want the heat on?" Noah asked when she shivered slightly.

"Not really." *How thoughtful he was!*

Marcy and Brad were waiting for them in the churchyard when they arrived, and Candle thought they made a handsome pair. She hadn't apologized to Brad for standing him up, unintentional though it was, and she wasn't sure whether or not to do so now. Instead, she smiled at him awkwardly and made introductions all around.

"So," Brad said, holding out his hand to Noah, "you're the one who makes Candle forget Bach."

Noah's eyebrows raised as he returned the handshake, but before he could voice his puzzlement, Candle interrupted, "It worked out beautifully, didn't it, Brad? Exactly as I planned!"

"Then you're an angel and a saint."

"Speaking of which . . ." Marcy pointed toward the heavy wooden door. "We really should go in."

Since she was on familiar ground, Marcy led the way, chatting over her shoulder as she answered questions about the church building, which was made of coquina rock.

"Ko-KEY-na?" Candle repeated. "I've never seen anything like it."

"It's a native building material," Noah explained, "made up of coral and skeletons of tiny sea creatures embedded in limestone deposits. Beautiful, isn't it?"

"Very," Candle whispered her agreement since Brad had opened the wooden door.

Walking silently ahead, Marcy dipped her fingers in a water receptacle fastened on the doorpost then touched her forehead, chest, left shoulder, right, making the sign of the cross over her body. Brad followed suit.

Candle hesitated, glancing at Noah. Smiling, he shrugged. Not knowing what to do, Candle prayed, asking for a blessing on their worship with other Christians.

Close to her ear, Noah whispered, "You know what just came to mind? Deuteronomy 6. 'Love the LORD your God with all your heart and with all your soul and with all your strength. These commandments that I give you today are to be upon your hearts. Tie them as symbols on your hands and bind them on your foreheads. Write them on the doorframes of your houses and on your gates.' I never thought of those words in the New Testament sense until now."

Candle nodded. She didn't understand, however, what her friends were doing. Before entering the long wooden pew, Marcy curtsied, and Brad bowed low, bending his knees—to what? The cross? The crucifix? The small statue of the Virgin Mary?

Candle felt bewildered. Something in her withdrew from bowing to images, even if they portrayed Christ himself. She slipped quietly into the pew, kneeling in prayer with the others. *Oh, Lord, help me to be open to your presence. Help me to understand.*

Since the mass itself centered around the Eucharist, the sermon lasted only a few minutes before the sacrament began. As people went forward to the altar railing to receive the bread and wine, a young woman accompanied herself on the guitar, her rich voice singing the familiar "Amazing Grace." When the beloved hymn had ended, Candle felt like applauding. Never had the words of that favorite song made so much sense to her.

The mass ended with Mozart pumped out on enormous organ pipes. Candle felt certain she could glide out on the music, her feet not touching the floor! But her heels clicked to earth when, again, Marcy curtsied beside the pew. No, Candle realized, she could not ignore her disturbing feelings. She had to ask.

"Marcy," she blurted, as soon as they'd reached the churchyard. "Why did you curtsy beside the pew?"

"Curtsy? Oh, genuflecting. When you genuflect, you bend your knees in respect. Some people touch their left knee to the floor so it's not quite the same as a curtsy."

Candle felt impatient. "But why? Or, rather, *what* are you genuflecting to?"

"Christ, of course."

"You mean the crucifix?"

"No," Marcy said. "To Christ. He's present, you know. Remember he said of the bread, 'This is my body,' and of the wine, 'This is my blood.' Well, we believe he meant just that. Through some mysterious, miraculous way, he is actually in the Holy Eucharist, ready to be received in mental, spiritual, and physical communion with his people."

"Oh!" Candle exclaimed.

"My church takes a similar position," Noah injected, "although I expect that some people never think of it that way. Instead, they view communion as a *memorial* service."

Candle smiled. "I think I followed that."

"Enough theology on an empty stomach," Noah insisted. "Anyone ready for lunch?"

Marcy looked at Brad. "Coffee, maybe?" He nodded, and she hastened to explain. "We had already made plans to lunch with Brad's parents before we knew you were coming." Her cheeks pinked, and Candle couldn't help but smile.

In a small restaurant overlooking the Atlantic, the two

107

couples chatted over their coffee, scarcely aware of the view. Noah declined ordering lunch until Marcy and Brad had to leave, and now he riddled her with his own questions.

"I've never understood Mary's position in the Roman Catholic Church," he admitted.

"And I've never understood why our separated brethren cast her out," Marcy countered good-naturedly. Then, seriously, she said, "Most people recoil from mention of Mary, even though they agree she was blessed and that she was the virgin mother of Christ. Apparently our devotion to Mary— our recognition of her—is misinterpreted as worship, and frankly I can see why some people think that. But, the way I've come to look at it is Mary is a symbol of the mother church, a representative of all Christian people. She was the first Christian—Christ in one. And he came into our lives because she allowed him into hers. Am I making sense?"

Noah smiled. "Very much so. Thanks, Marcy."

"It's a touchy issue—even within my church." Marcy glanced at her wristwatch, then at Brad. "I hate to *not* eat and run, but we really should be going." She bent to kiss Candle's cheek, taking the opportunity to whisper, "Your reverend is all right!"

Candle flushed as she waved goodbye, and when she looked back at Noah, he was staring at her, thoughtfully. "I like your friends. And you were exactly right."

"About what?" she asked.

"St. Michael's was the place to start. But . . ." he hesitated, frowning. "I've never thought of myself as prejudiced, but I'm wondering now how many other areas I've closed off." Noah glanced down at his menu then and directed his words toward scallop and veal prices. "You're looking particularly lovely today."

Candle almost didn't hear him, and when she did, she was

sure she hadn't. Her thank-you bounced off her own menu, upon which it was impossible to concentrate! Was Noah revising his opinion of attractive women? All women? Or was he merely acknowledging his need to open up to new things? Either way, it was a big step—and a vulnerable one. Candle found herself praying for the Lord's protection over him.

"The seafood here is excellent," Noah was saying now. "So is the fruit plate, if you'd like something lighter."

She closed her menu gratefully. "The latter would be fine." Had he asked, she couldn't have told him one thing on the list.

Casting her thoughts out to sea and allowing them to drift slowly back to her, Candle scarcely noticed when the waiter, at her elbow, refilled her coffee cup. Silences with Noah were so companionable, she was apt to get lost in them. She said as much to him now.

"I won't let you get too far away," he said, sending Candle's pulse racing. But then she convinced herself she was reading too much into his words.

The fruit plate arrived moments later, so artistically arranged that she hated to disturb the slender melon slices and enormous strawberries set in a circle. "Don't tell me these are Florida-grown."

"Then I won't. But they are," Noah said.

Candle laughed. "You're Florida-grown, too, aren't you?"

Noah nodded. "Born and raised in this area, and I can't imagine living anywhere else. But what about you? I hear the trace of a southern accent, don't I? What . . . North Carolina? Tennessee? You said your family moved when you were young."

She smiled, pleased that he'd remembered. "North Carolina originally. My parents still have a mountain cabin there for family vacations."

"A close family, I bet."

"We have our ups and downs and hard-headed opinions, but, yes . . . I'd call us close."

"Don't you miss that? I mean—" Uncharacteristically he faltered. "Don't you want that again?"

"I suppose."

"Then why aren't you married—or involved with someone?"

"It's not that I haven't been asked," she answered lightly. "In fact—"

"Brad?" he interrupted.

"No, why would you think that?"

"I detected an undercurrent between you two," Noah admitted.

Candle's lips parted in surprise. How could she explain the crazy set of events that had flung Brad and Marcy together? It was enough that Noah knew of her stupidity in getting a blistering sunburn! But to let him know that she'd forgotten Brad, forgotten Marcy, her best friend, forgotten Bach because . . . because . . . *Because the first time I saw you, Noah, I knew our relationship would be different, would be special . . .* There! She'd admitted it to herself. But she certainly would not admit it to him. He wouldn't want to hear.

And so she merely shrugged in response to his question. Apparently, the gesture antagonized him more than her silence. "I see," he said, his face hardening, his voice tight, and Candle knew he didn't see at all. He waved aside the waiter's attempt to refill his cup again and asked for the check instead. "You and Marcy are good friends?"

"Very."

"And you're not interested in Brad?"

"Of course I'm *interested* in him!" Candle retorted. She didn't like Noah's tone of voice or his insinuations. Naturally she was interested in *all* of her friends, and if Noah couldn't understand the innocence of that, too bad!

As they drove down the beach in a quietness no longer congenial, Candle felt saddened by the loss. She tried to pique his interest in a pelican whose pouch bulged with a fresh catch of fish, but Noah didn't respond. Why was he so angry? Was he jealous? Or, worse, did he think her disloyal to Marcy?

Tasmine had been disloyal—unfaithful—and Candle chided herself for not making the connection sooner. Ever since she'd begun to understand Noah's wife and his marriage, the exotic beauty posed no threat to her. But she'd made the mistake of forgetting Noah's old wounds.

Perhaps if she explained to him now that she was delighted for Marcy and Brad—delighted for her part in their meeting—it would help.

"Noah," she began hesitantly, "the undercurrent you mentioned between Brad and me . . . It's not what you think. I mean, we did go out, but . . ." No, this was starting to sound like she'd been jilted, Candle realized. She waited until they'd pulled into the curved drive and Noah had switched off the ignition before resuming. "Marcy is the dearest friend I've ever had, and I'm very, very happy for her and Brad. They do get along well, don't you think? And I wouldn't want it any other way. I . . ."

Lightly, Noah placed a shushing finger across her lips. Then his eyes softened, sweeping her face. The fingertip moved, delicately tracing the pattern of her mouth, and he leaned toward her, closing the distance until they were only a breath apart.

"Forget him, Candle," he said as his lips brushed hers.

It wasn't really a kiss, she thought—at least not a romantic one—and she supposed Noah meant to comfort. But, with her own emotions racing, that irked her, and so she snapped, "Is that supposed to make me forget?"

Noah looked stunned, then angry. Pulling her against him, his lips came down on hers, hard.

Overwhelmed, Candle restrained herself before giving in to the kiss. This was what she'd wanted, wasn't it? Hadn't she practically goaded him into it? And so she might as well enjoy it. Her arms went round his shoulders, and for a moment, she thought she'd drowned. Then she felt like she was being sawed in half. "Noah!" she gasped, pulling away. "My seat belt!"

Astonished, then amused, he released her and unbuckled the shoulder harness. Then he just sat there, looking at her.

"What are you thinking?" she asked, afraid to know.

"That you're . . ." Hesitating, he reached out and touched her hair, toying with it, caressing it against her shoulders. "Beautiful," he said. "You should let your hair down more often," but she wasn't sure whether he was referring to her coiffure or to their kiss.

"Noah—about Brad . . ." she started.

"Wasn't that discussion ended?"

She shook her head. "Not until you know that I stood him up! I didn't mean to—I simply forgot. But what I had planned to do was arrange for Marcy to go out with him instead, and as it turned out, that's what happened anyway."

Noah looked puzzled. "Why didn't you tell me this— straight out—at the restaurant?" His tone indicated disappointment in her—the very thing she'd been trying to avoid.

"Because I didn't want you to think that I was . . . that I'm a fluff head!" Then before he could come around to open her door, Candle got out of the car.

Noah caught up with her quickly. Grabbing her elbow, he spun her around. "How could I possibly think that of you?"

"I don't know! But you seem to think that women come in two fabrics—fluffed or starched—and I'm not either!"

"No one said you were!" he snapped.

Immediately she sensed his frustration as his hands closed and unclosed at his sides. Regretting that she'd pushed him into a confrontation—not with her, but with himself—she said, "I'm sorry, Noah."

"For what? For telling me what you think? For being a matchmaker? For kissing me?"

"Kissing you!" she protested. The next thing she knew, he'd be telling her she was chasing him! "As I recall, *you* started it!"

"And what were you? A lump?" he asked hotly. "I think, Miss O'Shea, you're entirely too forgetful." Then to refresh her memory, he scooped her into his arms.

Peevishly, she tried not to respond, but it was impossible. She kissed him soundly, with no regrets, until Mrs. Cousins opened the door.

chapter
10

IF THE HOUSEKEEPER'S REACTION WAS NEGATIVE, she did nothing to show it, hiding her opinions behind an impassive mask. She did, however, let Candle know that the reverend's Sunday afternoons were his own by pointedly asking him if he planned on resting—undisturbed—in his study "as usual."

When Noah nodded his assent and slipped off up the stairs without a word, Candle felt disappointed—and chastened. It wasn't that she minded being alone—she enjoyed her own company—but she had hoped for his.

Thirsty, she wandered into the well-equipped kitchen where Mrs. Cousins generously offered her a choice of soda, lemonade, or tea—hot or cold. She gratefully accepted a frosted glass of lemonade and started out the door when the housekeeper's voice stopped her.

"He needs rest, you know."

Candle smiled—Mrs. Cousins was being a mother hen again. She let the housekeeper know it was all right. She understood.

But the older woman shook her head. "Not physical rest—though, Lord knows, he could use that too. Sundays are his quiet time. I reckon you could say it's when he just listens."

"To the Lord?" Candle asked.

Mrs. Cousins nodded. "Not that he doesn't listen other times, mind you, but he needs Sunday afternoons for 'refilling and refueling,' as he says."

"How? With prayer? Bible study?" Candle was curious.

"You'd best ask him," Mrs. Cousins replied, turning back to the dessert she was preparing.

Candle leaned against a countertop of gleaming ceramic tile and sipped her lemonade while Mrs. Cousins sprinkled a generous handful of crushed pecans atop a torte.

"What about you, Mrs. Cousins? Don't you ever have a day off?"

The hand powdered with pecan dust stopped mid-air. "'Course I do!" she snapped defensively as though Candle had insulted their employer. But Mrs. Cousins obviously didn't think of Noah as her boss; he was family, and Candle understood that all too well. "I can take off anytime I want!"

Candle grinned. "But you seldom want to—right?" Impulsively, she pecked the wrinkled cheek, then setting down her emptied glass, she announced that she was ready for a nap.

In her rooms, which seemed truly hers—they'd never been Tasmine's—Candle drew back the pleated sheers that stood behind the heavy drapes. Salt spray filmed the jalousied windows, and she supposed that cleaning them was a never-ending job. Surely Mrs. Cousins didn't do that too! No— Noah wouldn't allow any employee to be overloaded. He looked for efficient people—the best for the job—and then he got out of their way and let them do it.

Gary never did that, she realized. Under the guise of caring, he kept projects—and people—well in control. Candle hadn't known she minded, but now she realized that was one reason she'd needed to get away.

Rolling out the slanted glass panes, Candle breathed in the cool salt air. Even the windows in Noah's house were the best for the job. Like tiers of small glass roofs, they let in fresh air but kept out all but the most persistent driving rains.

Suddenly she realized that she couldn't keep Gary out forever. Slipping off her pink silk, she hung it carefully in the spacious closet, then stretched out on the queen-sized bed. She'd have to write a chatty letter telling him of Noah's manuscript and hinting that she planned to stay in Florida at least until the work was done.

Then what? she wondered. What place would there be for her in Noah's life when his thesis and book were completed? Even though he wasn't taking a full year off from his ministry, he was, in essence, on a sabbatical, and she felt she'd scarcely seen him. What would it be like with him back on the job? Would there be time for her, for them?

Oh, what am I doing? she asked herself. Noah had expressed no interest in her. Or had he? Was his a kiss to help her forget, or to make her remember?

She recalled it now—the sweet firmness of his lips pressing against hers, his long fingers stroking her hair, her throat. *Stop it! He's in the next room talking to God, not himself!*

No, there was nothing about her attraction for Noah to be ashamed of, she realized. God was the author of love, and this? This could be a beginning. *Lord, help me to know!*

Funny, but she'd never prayed about her relationship with Gary. *Why, Lord? Did I know what you would say? Well, I'm asking for your light now.*

Heavy, her eyelids closed, and her thoughts drifted back to the mass at St. Michael's, where she'd discovered the church's beautifully poetic profession of faith. The words came back to her: "Lord, Jesus Christ, the only-begotten Son of God, born of the Father before all ages; God of God, Light of Light, true God of true God."

And she slept, thinking of the Light, thinking of Noah. A

beam of light swept the crevices, the dark corners, the inner knowings of her mind and heart, and shadows, stirred up, surfaced. The eerie forms took shape, gathering closer, closer.

She knelt in a church pew, surrounded by all the Christians who'd gone before, preserved in the very walls. Then that changed, and coquina rock—strong and inviting—sheltered her instead. Drifting, she was in the churchyard where the shadows had remained at bay until she wandered past. Something lurked, then jumped, seizing her. It was not a mass of people; it was a mass of darkness, prejudice, and martyred blood. She yelled. And then she was awake.

No sound came from her bed. But someone in the hallway was pounding on Noah's door, loudly calling his name. Candle hurried into a cotton duster and cracked her door to peek.

"Hush, Miss Townsend! I've told you! You cannot disturb the reverend." It was Mrs. Cousins.

"Oh, shut up!"

Candle's mouth dropped. How dare she speak to Mrs. Cousins that way! Apparently this was one of those spoiled young women who thought her status elevated her above other people. Well, she had another thought coming! Candle opened her door fully to give the brunette a piece of her mind. As she propelled herself, housecoated and unbuttoned, into the hallway, however, Noah stepped out of his study.

"Becky!" he exclaimed, but his dark eyes flitted over her and rested with amusement on Candle. She would have fled in embarrassment, slamming the door on them all, but Noah stopped her.

"Miss O'Shea, as soon as you've, uh, *dressed*, would you join us downstairs?"

Mortified, Candle clutched the thin cotton wrapper around her, wishing she could disappear as quietly as Mrs. Cousins had done. Speechless, she started to shake her head, but Rebecca Townsend's tone stopped her.

"Do we need her to take notes?" Rebecca laughed, but there was no music in the sound.

That did it! "I'll be down shortly," Candle said firmly. Then flushing hotly, she retreated to her room.

Leaning against the closed door, she let go her irritations. So that was Rebecca Townsend! No wonder Irene couldn't avoid her! Or Noah. And now it seemed that Candle herself was stuck. She'd make the best of it, she thought. Then suddenly she knew what to do.

Marching into the bathroom, she rinsed away the traces of sleep and patted her face dry with a lush towel. Then she opened her makeup case. Inside, the neatly arranged contents offered her the scope of an artist's palette. Most of the items she'd rarely used since she preferred merely to enhance her natural look, but now she was glad she'd experimented with new products from time to time. Several samples from a friend who marketed cosmetics remained uncapped, and Candle scanned the labels quickly. To her relief, she discovered that one unopened bottle contained a cover-up foundation heavier than the sheer makeup she usually wore for color-blending and protecting her skin. She'd had poor results in protecting herself from the sun, so far, but she hoped this would make the half-peeled patches vanish.

Shaking the sample bottle, she uncapped it, then dabbed dots of the ivory-cream liquid on her forehead, cheeks, and chin. Stroking lightly, she smoothed on the color that matched her own. With her complexion restored, Candle gently outlined her eyes with a soft brown pencil, then brushed a darker brown mascara onto her long lashes, making them appear even thicker and longer.

Since her afternoon nap had left her upper lids slightly

puffy, she reduced that effect with white eye shadow, lightly applied. Then, midway in the crease of her eyelids, she stroked on green shadow, that matched her eye color, bringing it down to the edge of each eye. The results made her wide eyes look even wider.

On the apple of each cheek, she brushed on a triangle of brownish-pink blush, ending with a dry dab on both earlobes. The color, she suspected, was a subdued version of the shade she'd naturally turned when Noah had caught her in the hallway!

What would he think of her now? She was pleased, she decided, as she stepped back for a critical look in the mirror. Perfume! She rummaged through the case and selected a heady blend, then used it sparingly on pulse points. She hoped she allowed enough time for the fragrance to set, but not wanting to risk otherwise, she moved toward the closet, waving her arms wildly.

She'd already decided to wear her two-piece satiny hostess set, partly as a statement to the uninvited Miss Townsend and partly because friends had told her she looked smashing in it. It was flattering, she knew. The rust color matched her hair, and the black mandarin collar framed her slender neck well.

Slipping on the jacket, which accentuated her figure, Candle fumbled with the braided black frog fasteners, thinking they were as elusive as the real creatures of that name. She hoped she wouldn't botch this now by getting nervous. The slacks, however, went on easily, laying flat against her stomach and trim hips. A pair of high-wedged sandals completed the outfit, and Candle headed back to the bath.

If she'd had more time, she would have done up her hair, but Noah had said he liked it down. Vigorously, she brushed out the tangles acquired in sleep, then back-combed for added fullness. There! That would have to do. Taking a deep breath to steady herself, she threw back her shoulders and glided downstairs.

On the landing below, Mrs. Cousins almost dropped the tray she was carrying when she saw Candle descending. "Well, I declare! If you don't look spiffy."

"Oh, thank you, Mrs. Cousins. It helps to have an ally. I haven't overdone it, have I?"

The housekeeper sniffed. "If you ask me, that Miss Townsend is the one who overdoes—pushing her way in here so high and mighty."

Candle placed a stilling hand on the woman's shoulder. "I'm sorry she was rude to you." Candle thought a moment. "Mrs. Cousins, why don't you take off for a while. I'll make sandwiches if anyone wants a snack, and . . ."

"And you'd be leaving *her* alone with the reverend?" Mrs. Cousins cut in indignantly. "I'll take care of my job, and you take care of yours."

Candle smiled weakly. She had a feeling that serving tea and sandwiches would be easier.

Inhaling another deep breath, Candle responded to Noah's call from the living room. Apparently he'd heard their voices in the hallway, and he'd risen from one of the sofas, starting toward the sound. When he saw his efficient, matronly secretary, however, he stopped dead, his face registering shock.

Candle walked steadily toward him, hearing his sharp intake of breath. She'd hoped he would return her smile, but as she neared him, a scowl creased his brow heavily, and his whisper was a hiss.

"I suspected you were hiding your light under a bushel, Miss O'Shea, but I never imagined you'd be quite so dazzling."

"Sorry if that bothers you, but we're not dealing with bushels or lights at the moment. Just fire," she hissed back. "*You* asked me to come down here, so here I am."

"You certainly are," he said, running his eyes over her slowly.

"Look," she said, feeling uncomfortable, "all you have to do is say so, and I'll go back upstairs! But I got the impression you wanted my—my *protection*."

"Who's going to *protect* me from you?" he asked, not unkindly.

"Ooh, you are the most infuriating, egotistical . . ." She hesitated, searching for another word.

Noah's eyes flashed. "At least you have some idea of who I am. Tell me, Candle—who did I kiss today?"

"Me, Noah. Don't let this get-up fool you! It doesn't change who I am any more than your clerical collar changes you." She hoped the latter was true.

"You're right." He rubbed his forehead as though he had a headache. "You just caught me by surprise—stepping out of a fashion plate."

"So, do you want me to stay or not?"

"I can't imagine any man telling you to leave," he said, and for a moment she thought he intended to make himself the exception. But instead he clasped his hand around her waist and steered her firmly into the living room.

Rebecca pouted. "Can't you two confine your *business* to office hours?"

"Noah and I had something to discuss. We didn't mean to forget our guest." She hadn't intended to stress the "our" so much, and a glance at Noah showed his eyebrows lifted. He said nothing, but as Candle took a seat next to Rebecca on the sofa, she thought she heard him chuckle.

Despite the switch in seating arrangements, Rebecca dismissed Candle as though she weren't there.

"Oh, Noah, you know how that Sonya Vaughn couldn't hold a job? Well, guess what? She's been trained to give *face-lifts* without plastic surgery! Even *working people* can have modern cosmetology perform miracles."

Sipping her tea, Candle choked. So Rebecca *was* aware of her. She cleared her throat, then asked, "Do you work, Miss Townsend?"

"Why would I want to do that?" It was such an honest answer, Candle took a second look at the woman next to her. Rebecca was much younger that she'd thought.

"A job can be very challenging," Candle said, answering seriously.

"Especially when it has *side benefits,*" Rebecca added under her breath.

"Noah is a generous employer, if that's what you mean."

"It's not, and you know it." Rebecca's voice was so low Noah couldn't possibly hear.

Candle felt herself flush. She wouldn't let this silly, young woman get to her! Across the room, her eyes spoke to Noah's, and he took the cue, asking Rebecca about her father's health. With half an ear, Candle listened to snatches of the resulting conversation, grateful only that it didn't include her.

What did Noah expect of her? she wondered as she snuggled deeper into the down-filled cushions. If he had wanted her to rid him of this uninvited guest, she'd surely disappointed him. Well, it was his problem, not hers, and for a moment Candle resented being caught awkwardly in the middle of it.

After a while Mrs. Cousins appeared with a silver tray of cucumber sandwiches and a fresh pot of tea. She set the tea service—was it deliberate?—in front of their guest, while offering around the light refreshments.

Candle took one of the dainty sandwiches then turned, startled, when Rebecca asked if she could refill her cup.

"Why, yes. Thank you."

With an angelic expression, the younger woman slid closer to take Candle's proffered cup, which she filled dangerously near the brim. Then balancing the saucer precariously, she handed the cup back to Candle. As soon as her fingers had touched it, Rebecca let go. Hot liquid splashed onto Candle's lap and dripped down the sofa.

"How clumsy!" Rebecca exclaimed as though she'd had no part in the mishap. "Good thing you have leather cushions."

But Noah, who'd shot across the room, wasn't listening. "Are you scalded?" he asked anxiously.

"I'm not sure." Candle tried to laugh. "If you two will excuse me . . ." She rose gracefully and without looking back walked, chin tilted high, to the kitchen.

Noah followed, leaving Mrs. Cousins to mop up the sofa. His scowl had returned as he pressed a cloth, wetted down with cold water, against Candle's hip and thigh, then his face reddened, and he handed the damp cloth to her.

"I guess you'd better do this," he said awkwardly. "But I'm afraid your outfit is ruined."

Candle flashed him an appreciative smile. "It doesn't matter," she reassured him. "The dry cleaners may help, but right now I think I'd better change."

"Will you come down again?" he asked almost shyly, and that boyish appeal tugged at Candle's heart. But she shook her head.

Her tone carried an apology. "I've been burnt enough for one evening."

"So you have," he said, and with his face a mask, he turned on his heels and left a soggy Candle with tears splashing, soundlessly, on braided frogs.

chapter

11

"IF YOU PLAY WITH FIRE, you get burned," Candle told herself stoically.

She'd peeled off the tea-soaked outfit and given it to Mrs. Cousins at the housekeeper's insistence, and now she misted her upper thighs and hip with first-aid spray. The coolness felt good against her inflamed skin. *It could have been worse,* she thought, thankful that the tea water wasn't straight off the stove.

Her conscience hurt her more. And her pride. Being honest with herself, she had to admit that she'd hoped to take Rebecca down a peg or two. But taking a young woman like that down a peg meant hammerlike blows, not cat-like digs, and Candle knew she didn't have it in her. She was grateful for that anyway; she had not liked her own cattiness.

The problem, she realized, was in playing Rebecca's game, and if she had stopped to think about it, pray about it, she would have known: only Rebecca could win at being Rebecca.

Wiggling into a multicolored caftan, Candle wondered if it'd do any good to go back downstairs, being herself and being the ally Noah seemed to need. She sighed. No, only a partner, a helpmeet, a wife could function in that role, and until Noah had managed to handle situations like this on his own, he wouldn't be ready for marriage again. The best she could do for him was stay put and pray, and so she did so now. *Help him, Lord, and, help me to forgive Rebecca Townsend!*

A light tap on the bedroom door interrupted her as Mrs. Cousins called her name. Inviting her in, Candle rose from her knees. She did hope the housekeeper wouldn't expect her to rejoin Noah, but those fears proved groundless. Mrs. Cousins had thoughtfully brought up a dinner tray, which she set on one of the bedside tables.

"Thanks," Candle said.

"Didn't think you'd be coming down. Can't say as I blame you. That woman . . ."

"Has she been here before?"

"Once, but I knew she was coming. Not like today."

Candle's heart sank. If Noah had been unable to discourage Rebecca before now, tonight might be no different. For a second, she felt tempted to intervene, and then she realized that word was a telling one: *tempted.* She'd already given in to the temptation once tonight to put Rebecca in her place, and she'd accomplished little—except to make Noah wary of her! No, she'd followed an inner leading to remove herself from the situation, leaving the outcome up to Noah and the Lord. To do otherwise would be an act of fear and faithlessness. *Courage. Faith. Trust.* She prayed the Lord would supply those in abundance.

Left alone to tackle her meal, Candle was hungrier than she'd realized. Buttered asparagus, not quite in season, graced one half of her plate, while thinly sliced roast beef, pink and tender, covered the other.

Candle assumed that Noah and his guest had the same succulent dishes set on the marble table, and the picture of them dining alone together jolted her appetite. But the delicate green stalks of asparagus were delicious, and Candle concentrated on enjoying every bite.

When she had finished, she debated on whether or not to leave the wicker tray in the hall, then decided against it. Mrs. Cousins shouldn't be expected to provide room service. Yet Candle wasn't about to go down herself until she was sure Rebecca had gone.

What if she doesn't go? She shook the thought away. Noah wouldn't allow anything to happen that he didn't want.

Candle looked with annoyance at her alarm clock. It was still early, and her afternoon nap had robbed her of the need for sleep. Wandering into her sitting room, she stared at the lively painting of fish Noah had bought for her. For her? She wasn't sure and didn't want to think about him anyway. She glanced away, but then the pair of dolphins caught her eye!

"No escape," she told herself dryly.

It occurred to her that the fish and the dolphins were not unlike the icons she had discovered at St. Michael's that morning. The painting, the sculpture reminded her of Noah and made her aware of his presence, his importance in her life. At St. Michael's, the cross, the crucifix, the small statue of Mary, the stained-glass pictures, even the music pointed to Christ, reminding her of his presence. The problem with symbols, however, was when one didn't want to remember, when one was trying to forget.

It'd been so easy to push Gary out of her mind. There'd been few icons between them, and even less devotion. Ironic, then, that Candle needed to fill her thoughts with him now.

She had procrastinated long enough about writing him, and so she sat down at her desk, mentally composing a letter. Uncertain about her future, she wasn't ready to resign from her New York job, but she felt she should at least hint at the possibility. Gary would accept that better than he would her refusal of marriage, but that too would have to wait. She simply wasn't ready to deal with that emotional upheaval. Nor did she want to burn the bridges still connecting her present and past—especially when the future seemed so uncertain.

In other letters, she'd told Gary quite a bit about Florida but little about her present job. She began now by describing the work in full. Whenever she could, she avoided mention of Noah and of living in his house, but eventually she explained the premise of his doctoral thesis and her own idea of developing it into a book for general readership.

When she'd stressed the book's importance and its marketability, Candle reminded Gary that she knew Woodward Publishing well. Even though the company seldom purchased manuscripts of a religious nature, this was just the type to succeed, so naturally she wanted Woodward to have first chance. This was a real find, she told him with enthusiasm, a gift. And she hoped he wouldn't be too disappointed that its writing meant her need to stay in Florida longer than expected.

When she had finished, she read the letter over, praying that the Lord would show her anything she needed to add. The thought came to her that she was playing it safe—which didn't please her—yet she couldn't bring herself to clobber Gary with bad news! What would she say? That she couldn't marry him until she remembered why she thought she might? That she had no intentions of returning to her old job, if . . . If what? If Noah wanted her to stay?

Somehow she didn't think Gary would be too understanding of the situation here. So she put the letter aside while she typed up the outline she'd completed for Noah's book. Perhaps if Gary saw that, he'd be swayed by the book's saleability, and his interest in the project would make him supportive of hers. She doubted it, but it was worth a try. She'd like to leave him with something.

The time and Candle's fingers flew as she typed, getting the book proposal in order. She'd finished the last page and was packaging up the manuscript and letter in a manila envelope when someone knocked on the sunroom door.

The wicker tray! She'd completely forgotten it, and now poor Mrs. Cousins had come for it herself. Throwing the sealed envelope onto her desk, she called for the housekeeper to come in, apologizing before the door even opened. When it did, Noah stood on the threshold, shaking his head.

"I heard you typing," he accused. "Is it so hard for you to take a day off?"

"Not usually," she said, stressing the fact that this wasn't exactly a normal day. "I had a personal matter to take care of, but it turned out to be more of a chore." Surely he could relate to that. "Anyway, I'm finished," she said breezily, clearing her desktop and turning down the addressed side of the envelope. Noah probably would not be impressed with the work she'd put together on his behalf, and if he knew the touchy situation she was in with Woodward Publishing, he'd probably tell her to find another company or, worse, forget the book altogether.

"How's the burn?" he asked, gesturing so that she half expected him to come see for himself.

"I'd forgotten about it," she said truthfully, her mind on other things. "The first-aid spray Mrs. Cousins brought me did wonders. I—I thought you were she now, coming for my tray. I'd meant to bring it down myself. . . ."

"I'll get it," he offered, crossing the room at the same time. "Did you enjoy your dinner?" he asked, returning.

She nodded. "Did you?"

"Not particularly."

"Oh."

It was an awkward conversation made more ridiculous by Noah's balancing her tray like a waiter as he leaned against the sunroom door.

"You're staring at me," she said.

"Am I?" he asked but didn't stop.

Candle sighed. She supposed his evaluating look was to be expected, considering his astonishment over her appearance. She wished she knew what he was thinking. Then, on his own, Noah chose to tell her.

"You're a beautiful woman," he pronounced at last, "but I assume you're aware of that."

She lifted her chin. "I've been told what others think. Personally, I consider blondes more attractive."

He gave a half smile. "Really?"

"Or—or *brunettes* like—like your Miss Townsend," she stammered.

"Jealous?"

"Why should I be? She's nothing to me."

"Nor to me," Noah said. Setting down the tray, he came closer. Hovering over her, his dark eyes teased, retracing the patterns of her face, her hair, her . . .

"Noah!" she protested, "I get the feeling I've made you uncomfortable tonight, but you're making me more so! If you don't mind, I'm going to go wash my face!"

As she brushed passed him, he stopped her, pulling her to him. "And then what? You'll slick back your hair and lose yourself in some tent of a dress?"

"Yes! Why not? Isn't that what it takes to make you see me as a person?"

"See you as a person! How can I when you're not honest with me?"

"Listen, Noah, *you* jumped to conclusions. *You* saw what

you wanted to see! But I needed a job, and I knew I could do this one well. So, you be honest with yourself. Would you have hired me if I'd looked then like I did tonight?"

"Probably not," he admitted, "but . . ."

"But nothing! I've done a good job!"

"A good job at what—pretending?"

She pulled away. "Maybe so. And that was wrong of me. But doesn't it strike you odd that I *had* to? I'm not Tasmine, Noah. Or Rebecca. I'm me. I'm the person you hired to help you, and I can't think of anything I'd rather do. But—you tell me. Do you *value* the help I've been? Do you value me? If not, I have no choice but to pack my bags and leave."

Lightly his hand touched her cheek, then dropped away. "Don't go, Candle," he said in a flat voice. Then picking up her tray, he left the room.

chapter
12

FOR SEVERAL DAYS, they kept their distance—working at their own desks, checking on necessary details through the intercom, eating meals alone. Candle preferred it that way, and apparently Noah did too, although neither of them had discussed routines or their need to work apart. The few conversations they had were strictly business, which was ironic, she thought. It seemed a bit late for that.

Nevertheless, the space between them provided a rest, a reprieve from the intensity of a relationship that had gotten out of balance. It enabled Candle to concentrate on her work. At least while working she felt successful, competent, accepted. With that confidence, the cushioning distance, and the certainty that God was at work in her life, she was able to cope. But it did no good, she found, to dwell on the future, on what she wanted her relationship with Noah to be. Resolutely she turned that matter over to the Lord, praying for Noah's healing and praying for his acceptance of her as a person, regardless of what she could do or how she looked.

She dressed for herself, rather than him, choosing the colors and styles that made her feel good about herself—nothing showy, nothing drab. She chose colors that complemented her own coloring, and outfits that fitted well, but weren't revealing—the way she'd always dressed before she had hidden her looks from Noah. Even though she saw little of him that week, she kept her hair down—loose and flowing like he preferred, but with the edges tucked back behind her ears to keep it out of her face. To suit herself, she wore a light touch of makeup that awakened her wide-set green eyes and moistened her lips with gloss more than color. The look, she felt, described her more than the plain person Noah was accustomed to seeing, yet the natural softness did not portray the type that had attracted Gary. He preferred, Candle realized, the very women Noah most avoided—women too unlike herself.

She wondered why Gary hadn't written—or called. She'd half expected him to phone as soon as her letter arrived, which should have been by mid-week at the latest. But then that wouldn't have given him time to respond by mail, and she had, after all, told him not to phone. Somehow, she knew that wouldn't stop him—especially if he were upset with her for the delay in coming home. But maybe he wasn't. Maybe he was pleased with the book she'd proposed, and he was waiting to hear from the marketing department about its long-term saleability. She doubted it, but one could hope.

On Friday, however, a postcard arrived, letting her know Gary was away on business. The scene depicted on the card denied that, but Candle didn't care. Her interest in his personal life seemed amazingly lacking, and she simply wanted to know—had he read the book proposal?

Since he made no mention of her letter, she supposed it hadn't arrived before his departure, and Candle felt a curious mixture of disappointment and relief. She hoped Woodward Publishing would accept Noah's book, yet she couldn't imagine staying on here indefinitely, while she and Noah worked as strangers intent on their own achievements. The atmosphere would have to lighten, or she knew she'd have to return to her old job, completing the work for Noah as she had time. But he had said, "Don't go," and that thread held her, waiting.

By the time the weekend arrived, however, she had begun to admit to herself that she felt lonely, and so she phoned Marcy at the office, hoping for her company.

"Oh, Candle, guess what Brad and I are doing this weekend! Going to Key West! Isn't that exciting? Brad has friends there, and so do I, and they've invited us to stay and, oh, I just can't wait. To see the sunset . . ."

And stroll hand in hand with someone you love. With conscious effort, Candle squeezed out the picture and expressed her delight, then got off the phone as quickly as she could. Marcy's euphoria contrasted too sharply—too painfully—with her own blue mood.

Saturday found her then, as on endless other days, alone at her desk with occasional interruptions and scoldings from Mrs. Cousins. Having successfully fixed her mind on the papers in front of her, she gave a little jump when the intercom broke into the familiar silence.

"Candle, are you there?"

"Yes," she answered, and in the long pause, she could hear him sigh.

"Did you want something, Noah?" she coaxed.

"Come into my study," he commanded brusquely before clicking off. He sounded displeased, and wondering what she'd done wrong this time, she hastened down the hall.

"No, nothing's wrong," Noah assured her as she entered the study. He motioned for her to sit down, and obediently, she complied.

"What are you trying to prove?"

Taken aback, she blinked. "Prove? I—"

"I said you'd done a good job," he interrupted irritably. "I said you were efficient. I said you were much more than a secretary—much more than I'd hoped—"

Surprised, she asked, "You did?"

"Yes!" He thumped his desk. "But my point is—stop it! Stop working every minute of every day! Stop holing up at your desk! Take a day off on your days off!"

"Is that an order?" she asked, not daring to smile.

Wearily he shook his head. "Just a request."

She leaned back in the chair. "Well, I have a request too."

"Which is . . . ?"

"Practice what you preach."

Noah shot her a dark look, then turning his back and folding his arms across his chest, he stared out on the sea.

"Beautiful view," Candle injected when it seemed he'd forgotten her.

"But not the only one." He turned around. "Have you seen anything of Florida except this?" he asked, gesturing toward the ocean and around the room.

"Not really," she admitted.

"Then you haven't visited St. Augustine—the oldest city in this country—or Cape Canaveral? And you haven't seen Edison's home at Ft. Myers with the original light bulb still burning! Nor have you seen Sarasota with its crushed shell beach and its gaudy but delightful Ringling mansion. Or Ringling Art with its massive biblical scenes portrayed by Reubens. Then there's Sanibel Island, colored with shells after a storm, and throughout the state, the springs . . . . Tarpon Springs with its sponges, Blue Springs with its wintering manatee." Coming closer, he checked them off on his fingers. "Need I go on?"

She smiled. "What about Disney World? Epcot?"

"Inventions for tourists!" he exclaimed. "Not that I don't

appreciate the craftsmanship, the genius that went into their making or appreciate the economy boost—I do. But did you know," he asked, settling on a corner of his desk, "at Key West people gather each evening to *applaud* the setting of the sun?"

"Oh." She shivered.

Having listened carefully to every word, Candle still wasn't sure what Noah was suggesting. A weekender? A romantic sunset for two? Or a drive around the state all by her lonesome. Neither choice suited the occasion.

Straightening her skirt, she rose to go. "I hear what you're saying, Noah, and you're right. I don't know exactly what I'll be doing this afternoon, but it *won't* be work. I promise." She wanted to extract the same promise from him but feared it'd be a hint, an unwelcomed invitation.

"Are we still on for tomorrow?" he asked as she opened the study door.

"Tomorrow?" she asked over her shoulder.

"Church. Your choice," he reminded her curtly, but his underlining tone said, "Please."

"All right—if you don't mind an architectural choice. There's a quaint little church somewhere between here and Marcy's," she explained, "and I've been wanting to go inside."

He laughed. "That's as good a reason as any."

"I'm not sure what denomination it is," she warned. "Does it matter?"

"Not at all."

"Good! Then I'll see you in the morning," she said cheerfully as she started out the door.

"Candle, wait." He put out a hand to stay her. "I— um . . ." He fidgeted uncomfortably but looked her in the eyes. "I heard what you said too, and, uh . . ." His hand combed through his black hair then dropped down, slapping a well-muscled thigh. "Look, I was wondering if you'd want to go with me this afternoon. I promised my grandmother I'd have dinner with her tonight, and I know she'd be delighted for you to join us. Cross Creek isn't too far from her place near Siloam Springs, and . . ."

"Cross Creek—Marjorie Rawlings's home?" Candle queried with enthusiasm. "I'd love to see it! Oh, but Noah, you must phone your grandmother to make sure she won't mind my coming."

He inspected the leather toes of his shoes. "When she called, inviting me to dinner, I, uh, mentioned that I'd like to bring you along."

Biting the edge of her lip, Candle reined in the edges of a smile. "You did? Well, I guess I'd better get ready," she said, then hurried off to freshen up. So Noah had mentioned her to his grandmother . . . . And his grandmother lived near Siloam Springs! So that's where Noah had gone on his mystery trip!

When she had changed into a cotton shirtdress with raglan sleeves and wide, muted stripes of cream and gray, Candle wandered through the house until she found Noah in the kitchen. Under Mrs. Cousins's supervision, he'd packed a picnic basket with snacks for the short trip. Enough to last for several days, Candle noted as she peeked beneath the lid.

"Fruit. Cheese. Hard rolls. Fried chicken!" She laughed. "Are you afraid your grandmother won't feed us?"

"Now don't you go teasing him," Mrs. Cousins fussed as she firmly shut the lid and handed the basket to Noah. "This man has hardly eaten a bite all week! A body's got to keep his strength up," she said, shooing them out the door.

Noah grinned as they headed for his car. "Guess *you've* been told," he said lightly, and Candle thought, yes, she had. She'd been told Noah had scarcely eaten!

Had his loss of appetite had anything to do with her, she

wondered as she slid into the car. But, on the road, she had little chance to speculate as the changing scenery caught her interest. Noah, again, proved a remarkable guide—pointing out this or that before she'd even time to ask. After a week of virtual silence, he seemed unusually chatty.

"My great-grandmother, Catherine Caldwell Jordan, came down this river, oh, back in 1895," he said as they crossed the St. Johns. "Come to think of it, it was about this time of year. Anyway," he went on, "she was orphaned and half-wild and dressed like a boy when my great-grandfather, Raff, found her. Called herself 'Cat.'" Noah chuckled, remembering.

"What do you mean, he found her?" Candle asked. "Was she lost?"

Noah laughed outright. "No, she was hitchhiking! Or the equivalent," he said. "She wanted to see Siloam Springs, so Raphael Jordan offered her a lift—on his raft! She was a feisty little thing, but he fell in love with her almost immediately."

For a moment they fell silent, and then Candle said, "I assume she made it to Siloam Springs."

Noah nodded. "Catherine Jordan was always one to accomplish what she set out to do. I remember her regard for the cracker people who lived in the forest here before it was a preserve. She couldn't bear the thought of one child going to bed hungry or poorly clothed. She invested her life in those people, while my great-grandfather dedicated his to protecting the land. Quite a pair, those two."

"H'm," Candle agreed. "They sound like my parents. Mom is a social worker for the county, and Dad's into environmental issues. He'd hoped to power their mountain cabin with solar energy, but they almost froze to death."

Noah laughed. "I'd like to meet him. Maybe he could give me some ideas on harnessing the Florida sun."

They crossed the dark and tortuous Oklawaha River, which

broke into light at Silver Springs; then passing through the lush green pastures of rail-fenced horse country, they entered the Big Scrub, thick with pines and oak and scrub palmetto. Beneath the paved but narrow road, creeks flowed lazily, while on the hard surface rabbits scurried and possums crept. As the car rushed past, a covey of quail shot into the air, scattered, then settled down again in the deep grasses.

Noah raided the picnic basket as he drove. "Rawlings's home is just a little farther," he said as he bit into a meaty chicken wing. Unlike him, Candle wasn't hungry, and she shook her head at this offer of a bite.

As the car slowed, she looked about—first at the hardwood hammock on the left and then at the wide but shallow front yard, trimmed and well kept. No one seemed to be around as they parked on the edge of the yard and got out—Noah opening her door.

"It's so quiet," Candle marveled, feeling she'd stepped back in time.

A gentle breeze stirred the oak leaves and slid down the steep roof of the small, one-story farmhouse with its guest cottage attached. The wood siding, painted white with its screened porch and windows trimmed in green, looked well tended, and Candle half-expected Miss Rawlings to step out and greet them. The feeling persisted as they entered the airy porch and found a sheet of paper scrolled into the vintage typewriter sitting on a round table.

"It's as though she's here," she told the ranger, a young woman, who'd asked them to sign the guest registry.

"Thanks—that's the way we want it," the ranger replied. "Come on, and I'll show you through the place."

Following the young woman's lead, they entered the living room with its wide-planked floor covered, in part, with an oval rug of floral pattern. Across from the fireplace, an oval table held an opened scrapbook, and it seemed as though someone had been settled in front of the fire, reading.

"The bathroom's in here," the ranger said pointing. "Miss Rawlings had the first indoor plumbing in the area installed with the money she earned in 1931 from the sale of her first Florida story. Then she invited the people she'd written about to celebrate, but they didn't use the new facilities: she had filled the commode with an enormous bouquet of roses!"

Touches of the author's humor and ingenuity remained even now, Candle noted, as they peeked into the main bedroom where a bowl hung from the ceiling, beneath a naked bulb. "That," the ranger explained, "was Miss Rawlings method of diffusing the overhead light."

The inventive, colorful flair extended into the kitchen where the author had delighted in preparing unique and delectable meals for her treasured guests. Vegetables hung from the ceiling to dry, and herbs and spices lined the countertop, reminding Candle of her mom's kitchen in the North Carolina cabin. On an oblong, wooden table sat a corn grinder, ready for use, and outside the kitchen door, a pump with bucket.

"I'll leave you two to wander around the grounds," the ranger said from the screened door. "You're welcome to come back inside. Stay as long as you like."

Thanking her, Noah and Candle exited into the sideyard of the farmhouse, then strolled about lazily, in no hurry to leave. It was easy to see why Marjorie Rawlings had left the city life she'd always known to come here to write undisturbed. Even with the company of bugs and occasional snakes and mice, the place had a serenity, a charm that invited creativity to flow as surely as the dark streams did, connecting the lakes. In finding her home, her niche, her subject matter, Rawlings had connected with the people, the land.

A certain wistfulness filled Candle as she and Noah wandered about the yard. A sad longing. She wished she belonged. She wished Noah would reach out and take her hand.

He'd been careful not to touch her, except with his eyes, and she wished she could discern his thoughts as they ambled quietly toward the car. Was he holding himself back? Or was he not interested? Was he afraid of himself? The past? Her? She didn't know where she stood with him—except that their relationship had possibly troubled him enough to disturb his appetite and that he'd wanted her along today for reasons of his own.

"Tell me about your grandmother," she said after they had climbed into the car and started down the country road in the direction from which they'd come.

Noah smiled, apparently thinking about this woman whom he clearly loved. "Cat named her 'Louise' after her mother, but she inherited both of her parents' zest for life and caring. Louise . . ." he interrupted himself, then added thoughtfully, "your middle name." He concentrated on negotiating a turn onto another narrow road. "She married my grandfather, Amos Seaton, just prior to the pre-Depression boom days, and after his death, oh, twenty years ago, she moved back into the house in which she'd been born—the house Cat Caldwell came to as a bride."

"So she's your father's mother?" Candle said.

Noah nodded. "Yet my mother is more like her—warm, gracious . . . If it weren't for Grandma Seaton's prayers, I doubt I'd be a minister today."

He fell into silence then, and Candle couldn't help but wonder how much Noah's father had opposed his leaving Seaton Industries for the church. From previous conversations, she'd learned that Mr. Seaton had died a few years ago of a heart attack, and Mrs. Seaton had gone back to her childhood home in New England. Noah saw little of her now, but they kept in touch, and Candle had heard the affection in his tone when talking to her by telephone. It pleased and relieved her that he showed closeness and warmth toward the women in his family—as though those relationships had given him a loving pattern not possible with Tasmine—and she hoped that any rifts with his father had long been healed.

It wasn't exactly the sort of question she could put to him, and so she asked him about Seaton Industries instead. Without much enthusiasm, Noah recounted factual data about the family business, now in his younger brother's capable hands, and from his voice and words, Candle sensed that there were no hard feelings—just disinterest in company affairs.

As they once again neared the St. Johns, Noah turned before crossing, winding along a narrow, paved road that ran parallel to the lazy, northbound river. No cars passed, yet the waterway itself seemed heavily trafficked. A rowboat clung to the shore, bobbing in the wake of a small but speeding cabin cruiser.

"Wasn't he going too fast?" Candle asked with a glance toward Noah.

He nodded. "Weekend boaters! One saber stroke of a propeller and another manatee is killed or maimed. They're such gentle, slow-moving creatures, they can't escape the fast boat traffic, and their numbers are steadily decreasing."

"What a shame! Isn't there something that could be done?"

"The river is posted with cautions and speed limits, but the St. Johns is big, and too many just don't care."

In quiet thought, Candle sat watching the river that disappeared occasionally behind palms and live oak and clumps of underbrush, and then the road curved, and it

CANDLE

vanished altogether. They drove a bit further, the land slowly ascending into gentle knolls where citrus groves had once replaced the palms. Killed by the frost of two severe winters and burned out by canker, few orange trees remained.

Noah gestured toward the horizon. "My great-grandfather, Raff Jordan, planted all of these groves sometime before the turn of the century, and they thrived until recently. The house his father built is just ahead—made of sturdy cypress. Who would've thought it'd outlive the trees?"

Candle looked in the direction Noah pointed, squinting to catch a glimpse of the old homeplace still hidden by ancient oaks and mammoth magnolias. When at last she could see the two-story structure with its wide, spreading veranda, she gave a little gasp. "What a wonderful old house!" For all of its size, it seemed cozy—homey—as it'd indeed been for generations, and once again, a wistfulness settled over her as they pulled into the long, oak-canopied drive. This house meant roots, belonging.

At the sound of car doors slamming, a woman in her early eighties appeared on the porch with a springy step, hurrying toward them. She hugged them both, hooked an arm through each of theirs—Candle on the right, Noah on the left—and chatting amiably, she led them up the veranda steps and into the house.

"Make yourselves comfortable, and I'll get some tea," Louise Seaton offered as she ushered them into the spacious, front parlor, but Noah wouldn't hear of it. Heading toward the kitchen, he left the two of them alone to get acquainted.

Candle settled onto a mint green, camel-backed sofa, assuming the overstuffed Morris chair was Noah's favorite and the well-cushioned oak rocker Mrs. Seaton's.

"I'm so glad you're here," the older woman said as she seated herself in the rocker. Her incredibly blue eyes appraised

Candle warmly. "Noah tells me how much help you've been on that work he's doing." The white head leaned forward. "I'm relieved he has you."

Her tone of voice indicated she wasn't just talking about the doctoral thesis, and Candle felt her cheeks warm. How much had Noah told this woman, whose eyes probed deeply to discern? How much could she see now? But her look was warm, accepting, and Candle relaxed under it, wanting very much to get to know this person who'd so influenced Noah's life.

They talked easily, laughed readily, until Noah came in bearing the tea, which he set on the butler tray table in front of the sofa. The talk ceased in a flutter of smiles, like two girls who'd been caught in the act of discussing some new boy at school, but Noah ignored it, good-naturedly.

"Am I pouring, or are you?" he asked his grandmother, and when she insisted she was, he called Candle over to the fireplace across the room.

"My family," he said, gesturing toward the mantel where daguerreotypes, tintypes, platinum prints, and autochrome portraits stood, scattered about. "This is Cat," he said, picking up an old black and white photograph of a young woman, bareheaded and smiling, aboard a steamboat.

"My mother," Louise Seaton said as Candle studied the print. "Even after I was born, she used to sing on the *Starlight* whenever it docked at Siloam Springs. The audience loved her—especially her song 'Dayspring,' but I always called it 'Hand Me Down the Dawn.' I don't suppose," she added, "that Noah told you he inherited her good voice?"

"No, he didn't." Candle made a face at him as she set the picture back on the mantel then picked up another—an autochrome, its colors faded now, of a young couple and a small child. "Oh, this is her again, so the baby must be you.

143

You have your father's beautiful blue eyes," Candle noted, seeing also Raff Jordan's resemblance to his dark-eyed great-grandson.

"He was a special man," Louise Seaton said, remembering. "Before I was born, he bought up all the land around Siloam Springs, and set what he could in groves managed by his friend, Wyatt Tate. Then he put Wyatt's brother, John, in charge of the old hotel. It's burned to the ground now, but I often thought my father—who had no interest in the hotel business—bought that grand old place just to give John something to do. Poor John had lost most of the use of his arm after a bout with polio," Mrs. Seaton explained, "and, well, my father considered the Tates his family. He was one to look after his own."

"Did you notice the gold locket my mother is wearing in that picture?"

"Yes, I did—it's exquisite. Isn't it the one you have on?" Candle asked, turning around for a closer look.

Mrs. Seaton nodded. "It was a family heirloom even then, and it only left us once when my mother sold it to help out the Tates. But my father bought it back, and she loved to tell me the story of how he placed it around her neck the night he proposed to her on the *Starlight*." She sighed. "Since I had no daughters or granddaughters, I'd always hoped it'd go to—" she stopped, looking flustered. "Now see how I rattle on! And our tea is getting cold."

They took their tea, toured the house, and then dined beneath the enormous chandelier Raff Jordan had purchased from the *Starlight* as a gift for his bride. So much continuity in this house, Candle thought, with so much caring, connecting one generation to another, and so much of the Lord evident in their lives . . . Yet something had struck her odd, she realized, as she and Noah headed home in companionable silence. Of all those manteltop photographs of Noah—as a child, as a young man, as a graduate from seminary—not one had showed him with Tasmine. *It was as though she'd never existed* Candle thought, *or as though she'd never belonged.*

chapter
13

SUNDAY MORNING DAWNED WARM AND BRIGHT, and rising early, Candle welcomed the day. Drawing back the drapes, she stood by the window, watching pink swirls tint the horizon until a palette of lavender and pale rose streaked the sky. Then suddenly the sun appeared, right where it belonged.

The sight gladdened her, and so did yesterday's memories, which came to her now, sudden, as the rising sun. Noah had *planned* to take her to his grandmother's—not to get her away from a desk—but to see how the two women would respond to one another.

Except for her observation of the mantel photographs and comments from Marcy, Candle had no real way of knowing whether Tasmine had accepted the Seaton family or they her. But she suspected that, in his rush of infatuation, Noah had given no thought to compatibility, acceptance, belonging, and that, wiser now, he had no intentions of making that same mistake again.

Hope rose within her like the skybound ball of light, marking a new day. Louise Seaton had accepted her immediately. Recognizing her as family? Recognizing that she belonged? Candle dared to hope so, simply because the recognition, the liking, were mutual.

The wistfulness she'd felt at the old Jordan homeplace was born of longing, and she'd instantly felt at home. She'd genuinely liked Noah's grandmother, and she'd liked Cat and Raff Jordan too. Wasn't that important? Wasn't it *crucial* to appreciate and value, not only Noah as a person, but the background—the heritage—from which he'd come? Wasn't it blessed to fit in—and know it?

As soon as that enormous thought came, however, a small doubt began to squelch it. What if Noah didn't see it in the same light? What if he'd just wanted company on a country drive? What if . . . ? She shook her head, refusing the doubts, and jumped into the shower.

When she'd dried her hair and dressed, she looked out again at the sun, quartered now in a mid-morning sky. The beach had begun to fill with cars and bathers, seeking tans, but her gaze went automatically to the tall figure, jogging toward the house. Looking up, he hesitated, breaking his pace, and then he waved. Candle waved back, smiling, then hurried downstairs to breakfast.

In the kitchen, she lingered over her orange juice, giving him time to shower, until Mrs. Cousins fussed at her that her eggs were getting cold. She took a small portion to satisfy both the housekeeper and her own grumbling tummy, but she ate as slowly as a picky, poky child. Despite the dawdling, she'd finished her meal before Noah arrived, his damp hair glistening like a raven caught flying in the rain.

His dark eyes scanned her before settling on the piping hot eggs and strips of bacon Mrs. Cousins set before him. "I'm starved," he announced. Then without glancing up, he said, "You're looking rested. Sleep late?"

"I watched the sunrise."

"Then country air must agree with you. We'll have to go again," Noah stated as he dove into the fluffy scrambled eggs Mrs. Cousins had prepared.

"I'd like that," she admitted, then sat quietly sipping her decaffeinated coffee while he ate.

When he'd consumed the last of the bacon, Noah excused himself to finish dressing for church, and, in the interim, Candle wandered back upstairs to reapply her lip gloss and comb her hair again. Her hand shook annoyingly, and she wondered if it'd always be like this—this surge of fear arising at the mere thought of going to church. No, not fear so much as the tension that comes from feeling threatened.

Having Noah beside her helped as she directed him calmly to the quaint little church she had in mind. But as they started inside, his arm about her waist, meant to comfort and steady, had a different effect. She was entirely too conscious of his closeness, she realized, as they seated themselves on ancient, wooden pews, and so she prayed that the Lord would turn her awareness only to him. *Heavenly Father, help me to worship you.*

She'd forgotten that it was Palm Sunday until the red-robed choir proceeded down the center aisle, waving branches and singing, "Hosanna in the Highest!" But the joyful acclamations and adorations turned to accusations, the praise to curses, the shouts to jeers, as the choir enacted the story of Christ's procession to the cross.

Watching the drama, Candle wept. She'd never seen anything like this, where the pain, the suffering, the rejection of Christ had seemed so real. She felt it—felt the immensity of all that he'd endured, and from the cross, she heard him say, "Father, forgive them," knowing he meant her.

The hand on her arm startled her as Noah offered her his handkerchief, and thanking him, she sniffed and dabbed at her eyes. She'd forgotten he was there.

"That was quite a service," he said as they exited into the noonday sun. "Your instincts were exactly right in coming here."

She smiled. "Next time, you choose."

"How about the next two times?" he asked and then explained. "I'd like to include a Wednesday evening service, too—if you don't mind."

She did, but she didn't want to say so, knowing that this research was important to him, and now she'd begun to see that it was equally important to her. Whether or not she *liked* it seemed as irrelevant as whether or not she'd like having a broken bone reset.

On the drive home, she caught Noah looking at her askance as though he were wrestling with thoughts of his own, and when they'd parked in the drive, he studied her openly. A question lingered around his eyes, and when she could stand it no longer, she asked, "What are you thinking?"

"Each church is unique," he said, and she felt he'd presented her with a riddle more than an answer.

"Do you mean the building? The drama? The ritual?"

"All of the above," he said, turning his eyes back to the road. "And maybe I mean the people. One never knows what to expect when no two are alike."

Alone in her room that afternoon, she thought about his words, thought about him. Sometimes she felt so very close to him; other times she felt she were on trial. She supposed most relationships went through a similar process, but with Noah, it seemed so intense.

How unaware she'd been of Gary these last days! How very little she knew about him. She hadn't meant to be unfair to him, and lately she'd regretted more than once not going ahead and making a clean break. But the book proposal waited, and she had to see that through, at least giving him first option on that—a small price when he'd wanted first option on her.

On Monday, she received a brief letter from him, written on hotel stationery, saying he'd be home by the end of the week. He suggested she join him, promising to lengthen his stay at the well-known resort where he was staying if she'd call and let him know she was coming. But her only phone call was to Marcy, making sure her friend had gotten home okay and had indeed had a good time.

Her own time, spent with Noah during the weekend, had lessened the tensions between them, and they worked together in his study, watching the manuscript take shape. The personality of each denomination became clearer to her on paper, and on Wednesday, the theoretical study became reality applied.

For contrast, Noah had selected a mid-week fellowship of prayer and praise, but as they entered the building, Candle's stomach lurched. The place reminded her of the church she'd known as a child, and suddenly she felt like a little girl, squeaking down the aisle in patent leather shoes. Heads turned at the sound. Frowns disapproved of her tardiness, but she managed to still her quivering chin and raise it high.

No one stared today. No one frowned. They were late, but no one minded. Packed into the modest-sized sanctuary, people stood with hands raised in praise and worship as they sang.

How different this assembly was from the church of her childhood! How different too from St. Michael's and the little church they'd attended Palm Sunday. For a moment the thought troubled her since she had no idea what to expect.

Beside her, Noah had already joined in the singing, and she felt lost, forgotten. How did he and the others know the words, the tune, when hymnals remained closed on the shelf-back of every pew? Sensing her predicament, Noah nudged her arm and pointed to a white screen set high above the pulpit. The words of a psalm were projected there, and finding the place, Candle added her soprano voice to the music surrounding.

The lyrics of a modern hymn flashed on the screen next, and when the lively song had ended, a wave of "Amen" and "Praise God!" rippled through the congregation. Behind her, Candle heard the musical voice of a young woman softly calling, "Jesus, Jesus," and in front of her, a man raised his outstretched hands in silent prayer.

After reading a passage of Scripture, the pastor of the church spoke on God's love as reflected through the Gospel of John. Then several people shared their testimonies of what that love had done in their lives. Healings of bodies, minds, and spirits were made apparent, and while the people responded with grateful "Hallelujahs," Candle lifted quiet thanks for the healing taking place in Noah's life.

The service ended with another psalm on the screen, and Candle recognized it as the one they'd read that Sunday at St. Michael's. The knowledge of that filled her with a warm sense of kinship, of lines crossing, paralleling, entwining, from one denomination to another, embodying together the full fabric of the Christian faith.

"Now I understand what your thesis is about!" she told Noah excitedly as they headed back to the car. She talked nonstop until he opened the passenger door. Then she slipped onto the well-cushioned seat and waited for him to slide behind the driver's wheel.

"I *understood* what you were saying before," she hastened to explain, "but today I really *felt* it—the importance of this unity amid diversity. It's a multicolored fabric of faith."

Noah beamed. "I'm glad, and I like your analogy." He put the car in motion and concentrated on backing out of the church lot. "You realize though that our next visit might not seem so successful."

Candle's smile faded. "Noah, I . . ." What? How could she explain to him that everytime she set foot inside a church, something inside trembled? He could never understand the amount of courage it took for her to go along with him, nor fully appreciate what a good sport she'd been about the whole thing.

Without her realizing it, Noah had pulled onto the shoulder of the road and stopped. His arm rested on the steering wheel, and when she turned to him, he was watching her thoughtfully, waiting, it seemed, for some struggle to cease.

"Candle," his voice gently broke the silence, "sooner or later, we're going to find that this fabric of faith, as you so aptly put it, has holes. But I suspect you already know that."

"Maybe that's it," she said, trying to keep her words light. "Maybe I've slipped through the holes!"

"That's absurd, and you know it! But somehow damage has occurred—damage that affects your ability to accept the church now."

Candle flung her hands in a gesture of emptiness. "I can't change whatever happened! I can't help how I feel!"

"That's true; you can't. But God can!" Noah insisted. "Or do you believe that his healing is only for those people who testified to it today? Always for somebody else, never for you?"

Candle smiled then, realizing that she had thought something of that sort. She'd prayed for Noah's healing and accepted the assurance that it was taking place. But she never thought to pray for her own needs, her own hurts to be healed. Her spirit soared, knowing he'd cared enough to claim God's power for her as she had for him.

"So. Where do we go next Sunday?"

"The place you most need to go."

He refused to give her any more clues, and Candle didn't press him further. But Sunday morning she awoke with a sense of foreboding that crushed her appetite and bagged circles under her eyes. Her makeup case restored her looks, but not her spirits, and even Noah's compliments on the green silk she'd worn didn't improve the way she felt.

She told herself that she was being silly, that she'd survived the other worship services, that she'd even enjoyed them. But this time, she knew, was different. This time she was going home.

She guessed even before Noah told her. He was taking her to the denomination of her childhood—the church she'd spent her adult life avoiding. Once there, she wanted to run. But his presence, his understanding when he couldn't possibly understand, calmed her, and she steeled herself for what had to be.

Lord Jesus Christ, Son of the Living Father, have mercy on me. Lord Jesus Christ, Son of the Living Father, grant me peace.

Where had those words come from? The missal at St. Michael's, she supposed, but regardless, they had a comforting effect, and she found herself relaxing as the refrain echoed in her head and soul.

"It'll be all right." Did Noah say that? Or did she think it? She glanced at him, grateful for his reassuring smile.

It seemed natural for him to hold her hand as they entered the sturdy brick building so like the one of her childhood. The pews had seemed endless then, the pulpit higher, the stark walls whiter, glaringly bright. The people had been taller, the preacher louder, the threats of hell fierier, glaringly bright.

She shuddered, and Noah put his arm around her, drawing her close on the wooden bench. Inside her, warmth exploded—not the warmth of searing condemnation or spearing lightning bolts of false guilt—but the warmth of tender mercy, of gentle rain. She didn't realize she was crying until Noah pressed a handkerchief into her hand.

A flood of forgiveness and acceptance washed through her, and when they stood for the familiar hymns, she could join in. She listened to the sermon, which made no mention of Easter or the risen Lord. Instead, it matched the fire of her remembrances, but, unlike the vulnerable child who'd been scorched unmercifully, Candle could hear what was being said and know that it was part of the truth, part of the whole fabric.

"Was I wrong to bring you here?" Noah asked somewhat anxiously after the service had ended.

"No." Candle patted his arm. "It was needed—just as reminders of God's judgment are needed for some people."

"And you?"

Candle laughed. "I think I have a vivid picture of wrath— enough to last a lifetime."

As they headed back to the beach house, a troubling note descended. She knew that she didn't belong in the church in which she'd grown up, but without it, she was orphaned. She didn't belong anywhere.

Mrs. Cousins was waiting for them with a message from Trinity. Noah's church. Noah's home. And another foreign species, Candle realized with dismay.

"I couldn't make sense of what he was saying, he rambled on so," Mrs. Cousins said now.

"Who?" Noah asked.

"That young fellow who's been filling in for you. Jacob somebody."

"Jake? Does he want me to call him?"

The housekeeper waved her hands impatiently. "No, he wants you to come. Said he'd wait at the church till you got there."

Noah frowned. "Jake wouldn't bother me unless it were important. I better go." He held out his hand to Candle, brushing her fingertips with his own. "Come with me?"

Involuntarily, she drew back, and Noah's hand dropped. "If you'd rather not . . ." he said coldly.

"No. I mean, yes! Give me a minute to freshen up," she said, flustered.

Everything was happening too fast, and she wished she had time to rest, to think. Instead she hurried up the stairs, promising Mrs. Cousins that she'd have a quick bite before she left, promising Noah she'd change into something more comfortable.

Food and clothing were the least important items on her mind as she grabbed the first pantsuit she touched, a tailored beige twill. When she had it on, she automatically tied a silk scarf of creams, rusts, and browns around her neck and slipped her slender feet into wedge-soled beige sandals. Then she dropped onto a corner of the bed and laid her forehead in her hands.

She didn't belong anywhere.

The thought tore at her, unbidden, unresolved, and she wished it would go away and leave her alone. She'd done just fine all these years without any church in her life, and now it was neither fine nor settled.

Noah did belong. He knew where he was needed and where he needed to be. He fit and was spiritually fit because of it. He knew how he wanted to worship, whether or not he wanted icons, whether or not he wanted roots, order, ritual, or spontaneity. He knew. She didn't. And that made matters worse.

"Do I even *want* to belong?" she whispered to herself, and the question jolted her into an upright position.

Her answer was tentative, fragile, because she couldn't be

certain of what was required of her or what she'd receive in return.

"That sounds awful, doesn't it, Lord?" she said aloud, but she knew it was okay to wonder, to find out, and she asked his help in guiding her.

A tap sounded on the door, and Noah called her name.

"I'll be down in a jiffy," she said, then hustled into the bathroom to straighten her mussed hair.

The face in the mirror was wide-eyed and vulnerable. *Lord Jesus Christ, Son of the Living Father, have mercy on me. Lord Jesus Christ, Son of the Living Father, grant me peace.* Once again the words strengthened, comforted, reassured.

She had no idea what she'd discover, and all she could do was open herself to the search. But it had to be for herself—not for Noah—as much as she loved him. Of that anyway, she was certain. She did love him more than she ever dreamed possible.

Did he love her? Sometimes she thought he might—a word, a touch, a glance. But it could be the kindness, the acceptance, he bestowed on anyone—except for his kiss . . .

Tossing her hair back from her shoulders, she laid down the brush, then reapplied a tinted lip gloss. *Maybe love is enough,* she told herself, wishing it were true. Then, displeased with herself, she made a face at the mirror. She hadn't expected to visit Noah's church home before she knew where her own was or before she knew if she really wanted to find where she belonged. But this was the Lord's timing, not her own, and she trusted he would protect her from confusion. There was, however, no confusion about one point: whoever loved Noah Seaton would have to love the church as well.

With that thought clinging, Candle rushed down to meet him.

chapter
14

ALONG THE INLAND DRIVE TO LAKEMONT, stands of pine trees replaced the coastal palms, occasionally interspersed with surviving orange groves. Here and there, rows of ghostly trees and naked branches attested to the heavy frost of winters past as they stood, basking futilely in the sun.

An armadillo ambled slowly across the highway, and Noah swerved, avoiding it.

"What prehistoric creature was that?" Candle asked, and Noah identified it, then launched into one of his favorite topics—Florida wildlife. Relaxing against the car's plush headrest, Candle listened with interest. This strange state was so unlike what she was used to, yet its flat lands and unusual beauty fascinated her.

As they neared the town, which spilled over its small borders, gaily-colored houses dotted the landscape, bouncing sunlight off tiled or graveled roofs. The clement weather had coaxed roses into bloom, and children raced across manicured lawns not yet tall for mowing.

An archway of stately oaks shaded the narrow street onto which Noah had turned, and shadows danced on the pavement as a light breeze played with the gray hangings of Spanish moss. Between two stout trunks, a driveway cut through to a large parking lot that ended in a grassy lawn. On it stretched a one-story white building with vertical battens nestled among shrubs of varying heights.

"What a charming place!" Candle exclaimed, delighted. For some reason, she'd envisioned modern lines, sleek and expansive, but never a building, a setting, as cozy as this.

"You like it?"

"Yes, very much." She took Noah's hand as he helped her out of the car. "But I don't understand. Unless the size is deceptive, it couldn't possibly seat a thousand people."

"It doesn't."

"But I thought—"

"You thought everyone came at once?" He smiled. "That would be impressive. But we decided some time ago that several small services would provide more of a family atmosphere. That's particularly important here because members are often transplants in need of roots."

"What a wonderful idea!" Candle was amazed. "But isn't it more time-consuming?"

Noah shrugged. "It's worth it. The people know one another better and are more apt to communicate when problems arise." He stroked his chin, thoughtfully. "There's not the feeling here of being one of a number—lonely, insignificant. In fact, several have told me they've found their niche because so much is going on and their special talents are needed."

"On Sundays, you mean?"

Noah laughed. "Candle, this church does not sit empty during the week!" As they talked, they'd wandered around the church grounds, and now Noah stopped, pointing to a low cluster of buildings that stretched from the sanctuary in a curved wing. "Those rooms house a day care center, study groups, and more meetings than you'd care to calendar. On the street side is a community shelter for anyone in the area or passing through who needs food, clothing, transportation, or a temporary place to stay. It's funded by a tithe from the church's income, and somehow there's usually enough in the kitty to go around."

"Don't outsiders take advantage of that?" Candle wondered.

"Probably. But that's God's problem, not ours. He's the judge; we're only here to serve."

Across a covered walkway, they moved slowly toward the sanctuary with Noah still holding her hand. "I wish you could hear the choir," he said outside the door. "The director pulls all stops—Bach, Mozart, Wesleyan hymns, spirituals, folk music. The pipe organ can handle almost anything, but if a piece calls for a violin, we have a violin. Or a guitar, or drums, or a trumpet—whatever is needed."

Candle wrinkled her nose. "You hire musicians?"

Shaking his head, Noah grinned. "I told you, Candle, people find their niche. Not just in music either. Some members have a gift for teaching, for prayer, for crafts, for cooking a fund-raising breakfast, for organizing a bazaar. We have a librarian who loves being surrounded by books and an in-resident poet who carves a few artistic lines in the church newsletter, causing all of us to feel, to think."

"A place for everyone," she said pensively and thought this surely could include her. But did she want it to? "Can we go inside the sanctuary, or is Jake expecting you now?"

"Whatever he wants can wait a few minutes," Noah said, not unkindly, and Candle got the impression that this tour was more important.

Still she had to ask, "But what if Jake's news is urgent?"

"It can wait," Noah repeated firmly. He dropped his hand and opened one of the heavy double doors. "Rarely is

159

something so pressing that we have to be puppets jerked about on strings. God doesn't play that way. Believe me, I've learned that from hard experience," he added quietly.

Candle nodded her understanding, glad that he was following perhaps an inner urging rather than outer pressures. They stepped inside the sanctuary, and an "ah" of appreciation escaped her lips. Easter was remembered here, she saw, as she noted the mass of lilies covering the altar. But more permanent reminders caught her eye.

Stained-glass windows, backlighted by the afternoon sun, depicted biblical scenes and symbols, each portraying reminders of God's love. Huge wooden beams reached up, supporting a tongue-and-groove ceiling that had been left in natural shades of pine, and even the arc of the wood, reaching out to God and others, seemed to express a longing of the people.

It was a restful place, prayed in and over, and at that moment, a young couple sat, heads bent, in a front pew. Not wishing to disturb them, Candle and Noah slipped out quietly.

She would have liked to stay longer, sitting, seeking, and so it pleased her when Noah said the doors remained open for anyone with need to come.

"It's only a building, of course," he added. "We can talk to God anywhere. But there's something special about a place that has been filled with people's prayers and God's blessings. I often end my counseling sessions there, and those prayers seem to make more difference than anything I have to say."

Most of the counseling, he informed her, occurred in his office, and they headed in that direction now. They entered first a reception area, empty today, which faced the covered walkway. Behind that stood Noah's spacious office with its comfortable chairs and rows of book-lined shelves.

A small man with thinning hair welcomed them from Noah's desk, extending his hand as introductions were made. Although he was obviously relieved to see them, Candle sensed a nervousness about the man.

"I, uh, hadn't expected you both to come," Jake began, apologetically. "But maybe it's best." Flushed, he looked away.

"What difference does it make if Candle is here?" Noah asked with a hint of annoyance, and Candle felt her muscles tensing.

"I'm sorry, Noah. It's difficult enough to tell you this, and now it's doubly so."

"Maybe I should leave," she said and started toward the door, but a motion from Noah stopped her.

"No. Tell us, Jake. What's happened?"

The other man dropped wearily into Noah's chair. "Rebecca Townsend," he said simply, and Candle felt like bolting.

Noah's voice was cool, controlled. "What has she done?" he asked as though he'd anticipated a problem.

Jake exhaled audibly. "For several days now, she's been spreading nasty gossip, and you know how people are, Noah. They'll believe what they want to believe. A few are up in arms, but those who know you, who know Rebecca, figure she's airing some private beef."

Noah face was a mask. "What has she said?"

"That you two are, uh, living together."

"I'm not surprised," Noah said. And without another word, he slammed out of the office, leaving Candle standing there in a state of shock.

Jake invited her to sit down, and when she did, she realized her knees were trembling. So was her voice.

"I don't understand any of this," she said.

Jake didn't answer immediately, taking time instead to pour

her a cup of coffee. Then he sat across from her, his warm eyes filled with compassion.

"Candle, I'm sorry this had to involve you—especially since you don't even know the woman!"

"Oh, but I do!" She groaned, remembering the awful scene. Had she played the part of hostess too well? Trusting Jake to understand and to be of help to Noah, she described Rebecca's childish visit, then ended with her current concern.

"What will happen, Jake?"

"We'll probably get a few phone calls, lose a few members, and in time, it'll settle down."

"But what if Rebecca won't let it?" Candle asked anxiously.

"She may not," Jake answered truthfully. "That's why I called Noah."

"It's so unfair!" Candle exclaimed angrily. She shot from her chair and paced back and forth on the carpeted floor. "Does this church have no discernment? Is it so quick to believe what's hateful while being blind to what's good?" She'd turned to the window, unaware that the office door had opened. "If this is the way church people act, if these are the people of God, then I want no part in them!"

From behind, Noah's voice was low, barely audible. "If you're looking for perfection, Candle, then you're right. You won't find it here." Without waiting for her response, he held out his hand to Jake, thanking him for his concern, his trust.

Jake walked them to the outer door, assuring Noah that he'd do what he could to calm matters down.

"I'd hoped it would help if you talked to Rebecca. It didn't, I assume?"

For a moment, Noah looked puzzled. "I didn't call her, Jake."

"But I thought . . . where were you?"

"In the church—praying."

162

If the two men had forgotten her presence, Candle's cry reminded them. How long had she prayed for Noah's healing? How deeply had she wanted him to be open to forgiving and being forgiven? And now because of these awful circumstances involving her, involving the whole church, his healing was complete. But Candle ran to the car, feeling miserable, knowing that her own had just begun.

The irony of it didn't escape her, nor did the fact that the car doors were locked. When Noah caught up with her, he spun her around and held her tightly as she had wanted to be held—but not in the church parking lot!

"Noah! We're confirming people's suspicions!" she said, and he let her go with obvious reluctance.

"Can we talk about it?" he asked, handing her a handkerchief.

She sniffed. "Not now." She wouldn't know what to say.

On the way home, appropriately, it rained, and the steady stream thumping on the car softened the sharp edge of silence. Candle closed her eyes and fell sleep. A small jolt, a sudden clap awakened her, and when she looked about, she saw that Noah had pulled off the road while sheets of rain covered the windows.

"It won't last long," he said, staring at the dashboard.

The brief nap had revived her, and she remembered her prayer earlier that day, asking the Lord to protect her from confusion. It seemed he'd done anything but! Noah glanced at her then, his face questioning, and she found herself pouring out the turmoil pent inside.

"I don't know if I *want* to be part of the church—any church," she admitted. "It's too . . . too . . ."

"Painful?" he suggested.

She shrugged. "I suppose so," she said, although she hadn't thought of it like that. "But don't think that means I don't care about God or you," she added defensively.

163

"So what are you saying, Candle?" His voice rose above the storm. "You care only to the point of pain? Spare me! Anyone cares that much—even Becky."

She felt like hitting him! "I am not Rebecca or . . ." She bit off Tasmine's name through clinched teeth.

But Noah supplied it for her. "You're not my wife. Is that it?" His eyes flashed dangerously, but remarkably he held his voice in check, like the low rumble of thunder. "Do you think you're any better because you *receive* pain instead of *causing* it?"

Candle's jaw unhinged with shock. "I don't even know what you're talking about!"

Noah slumped back against the car's headrest and closed his eyes. "Of course you don't know," he said wearily. "I'm only beginning to find out myself."

She waited for him to go on while the curtain of rain slowly unveiled the windows.

"Expectations," he said finally, his eyes still closed. "The false expectations we place on other people are as damaging as accusations or bullying threats. We expect love, and when we don't receive it exactly as we'd wanted, we accept the hurt instead—the resentment, the anger, the unforgiving attitudes. Don't you see?" He turned to her, the light in his eyes searching deep into her own. "We cannot receive what's good and healthy while receiving ill will. We can't accept kindness when we're accepting unkindness. We can't take love while we're collecting hurts."

"Victor or victim?"

He nodded.

"Noah, I can't help how I feel!"

"I know that! But, Candle, you can choose what you want to accept and what you want to reject." He started the car engine and turned on the windshield wipers. "You don't have to be a victim."

She thought she understood what he was saying, at least she hoped she did, but she couldn't resist needling him. "Are you placing expectations on me, Rev. Seaton?"

"Maybe I am."

"Then I pray you won't be disappointed."

The rain and their argument had cleared the air, and, saturated with fresh hope, Candle's mind drifted through the stillness. What Noah had said made sense, and she wondered if he fully accepted his own words. No, God's words perhaps. God's ordering her confusion to rest.

And Noah's? Was he willing yet to accept her love? Or would he choose to ignore it if she offered it to him now? Ignoring it, avoiding it, was just another form of rejection, a subtler one, she realized, and no different than her avoidance all these years of the church.

Her thoughts stretched to the joy of discovery she'd felt at Trinity. The beauty of it stimulated her senses, and she wondered if other people were first drawn by the physical aspects of worship, of love. Body, mind, and spirit—the trinity of personhood. No relationship, whether with God, self, or others, was complete if one part were missing.

She had to admit to herself then, that her relationship with God had suffered, not because she'd shut him out of her mind or spirit—she hadn't. But she had rejected his body and her own by not accepting her need for worship and for fellowship with his people.

The thought astonished her, but the next one even more. Unless she accepted the Rebeccas of the church, the non-Christ-like people, she would be the one isolated, left out, as though she herself were the one rejected. Something in her rebelled against the unfairness of that predicament. Something struggled, then submitted and died. God never promised life would be fair. Christ and the apostles warned of suffering. Was this what that meant? Dying to the right to be right? Stepping away from wrongs?

God help me! she prayed. And then deliberately choosing his still will instead of ill will, she asked, *Lord, forgive me for accepting the hurts, the resentments, from those who aren't reflecting you.*

Was this repentance, she wondered? The word, she knew, meant to "turn away from" one way to another. *Lord, I repent of my responses! Help me turn away from wounds given and received.*

Her feelings hadn't changed, she realized. She still didn't have a church home, and she still wasn't fond of Rebecca. But neither did she wish the woman ill. She did, however, find herself filled with an enormous curiosity, a desire to understand.

"Noah, why did Rebecca spread those rumors?" she asked as though there'd been no gaps in conversation.

"Probably something I said." Whatever it was, he didn't look ashamed of himself.

Candle frowned. She couldn't imagine Noah's saying anything cruel, and Rebecca wouldn't understand sutleties or hints! Yet she'd left abruptly and was stirring up trouble like a provoked child.

Realizing she was learning nothing by her speculation, Candle finally asked, "What did you say to her, Noah?"

He maneuvered the Mercedes onto the highway that ran parallel with the ocean, then, matter-of-factly, he answered, "I told her I was in love with someone else."

"No wonder she was upset! Why did you tell her that?"

"Because," he said simply, "it was the truth."

chapter
15

CANDLE SAT, scarcely breathing, waiting, hoping, wishing he'd say more. But Noah seemed in no rush, except to get home. His foot pressed harder on the accelerator, and it occurred to her that maybe he was waiting, too.

Nothing would delight her more than to to turn to him and say, "Noah, I love you, too." But he hadn't said he loved *her*.

It was possible, she supposed, that there was another person in Noah's life—someone, perhaps, that she hadn't met. But Candle doubted it. When she'd met him, he'd been very clear about his disinterest in any romantic entanglements. Oh, that seemed so long ago! And now she'd met his grandmother. She'd seen his church, and she, of all people, should know what—or who—was most dear to him, even if that meant herself.

Still, to be sure, she supposed she could ask him who was the lucky woman. But that seemed too glib, too superficial, to say to a man whose feelings ran slow and deep. She loved him, and it suddenly seemed foolish not to tell him so—if only her voice would work.

"Noah, I . . ." she began hesitantly, then cleared her throat. Not the most romantic beginning.

He shook his head. "Don't say anything, Candle. Not yet. I certainly didn't mean to."

She scowled at him. "Why?"

He shrugged. "Some things take time. Can we leave it at that?"

She sighed. "All right. But would you . . . I mean, is there . . ."

Reaching over, he squeezed her hand, then turned into the circular drive. "There's no one else," he said as the car screeched to a halt beside a long, low limousine parked in Noah's usual spot. A bumper sticker labeled it a rental. "Were you expecting anyone?" he asked as he switched off the ignition.

She shook her head, uneasiness giving chase to the momentary joy, but even then, she had no premonition, no awareness of what was about to happen. When they entered the foyer, she was as stunned as Noah to see Gary Woodward standing there.

"Gary!"

"Well, it's about time! Where have you been? I've been waiting forever!"

"I—I didn't know you were coming," Candle reminded him, although she supposed she *should* have known—intuitively. "You got my letter?"

"Of course! What's this about your staying on indefinitely? And *where* are you staying? Here? I drove to the address I had of that friend of yours, but no one was home. I thought I'd check at your *business* address! You know, Candle, I never expected *you*—"

"This *is* where I work, Gary, and this is my employer—whose home you happen to be in—Rev. Noah Seaton. Noah—Gary Woodward of Woodward Publishing." As she made the introductions, she wished the parquetry were butter so she could melt into it. Noah's hot look could have made that possible. Nevertheless, he extended his hand cordially.

Gary returned the greeting. "Nice place you have here. Plenty of room for offices I would think."

"A study . . . a guest suite . . ."

Withdrawing his hand, Gary turned to Candle. "Then you are staying here!"

"I never said I wasn't. Does it matter?" she asked. He had no right to come here like this without warning, and, oh, his timing couldn't have been worse. Yet, she knew she'd been no help in avoiding this situation, prolonging the truth, prolonging her goodbyes. She should have told him weeks ago. But she hadn't.

"Gary, we need to talk."

But Noah answered. "You're welcome to the living room. I'll be upstairs if you need me."

"Thanks, Seaton, but I'd rather take my fiancée home."

Noah's face blanched. "Your fiancée?" He looked at Candle as though she were a stranger. "Miss O'Shea didn't tell me. Perhaps there's a lot she and I don't know about each other. If you'll excuse me . . ." He strode past her and up the stairs.

"Noah!" she called after him, and when he neither stopped nor answered, she whirled around. "I'm sorry, Gary, but I'm not your fiancée! And I'm not going home with you!"

"Calm down, Carrot Top! Look, let's go somewhere and have that talk. It's early for dinner, but I skipped that plastic lunch on the plane. A good steak and each other's company should make us both feel better."

"All right," she agreed.

Excusing herself to dress for dinner, she left Gary in the living room and hurried upstairs. It was still Sunday—the day Noah spent some time alone with the Lord—and he'd already had far too many interruptions. But since she had no idea when she'd return from dinner, Candle couldn't bear the thought of Noah's being locked into this terrible misunderstanding. He'd come so close to telling her he loved her, and even without the words directed to her, he'd made his feelings clear. But what did he know of her love? What had he thought when Gary had said she was his fiancée? She could set that straight, she hoped. At least she could try.

Lightly, she knocked on the door of his study, and when there was no answer, she tried again. Turning the knob, she cracked open the door and peeked into a darkened room. "Noah?" She switched on the light, but he wasn't there.

Thinking he might be resting, she slipped into the study and cautiously opened the door into his adjacent bedroom, rather than entering it through the hall. She didn't want to bother him if he were resting nor disturb his prayers, but there was no danger of that. The room was empty.

She'd never seen his room before, and a sweeping look now made her smile. Instead of lush carpeting, a rag rug partially covered the dark oak floors, and a beautiful old quilt provided a homey touch on the pencil post, walnut bed. A walnut nightstand, plain with white knobs, stood beside the bed, and on its top rested a brass, candlestick lamp and a large, black leather Bible. The pages were opened to Psalm 51 where Noah had underlined verse 10, "Create in me a pure heart, O God, and renew a steadfast spirit within me."

She hadn't meant to pry or to intrude upon his privacy, and when she realized she was doing just that, she quickly exited through the bath joining his room to hers. A noise in the sunroom drew her, and she rushed in to find Noah sitting at her desk.

"What are you doing here?" she asked.

"Why were you in my room?" he countered.

"Looking for you."

"Well, you found me." He leaned back in the swivel chair. "The problem is—you failed to tell me you'd found someone

170

else before coming here. Tell me, Candle, how long was this charade supposed to last?"

"It wasn't! It isn't! I know I've handled the situation with Gary badly—I seem to be doing that a lot lately—but I wanted him to look at your book. He is the head of Woodward Publishing, you know, and he is still my employer!"

"Candle, the man said he's your *fiancé*!" Noah reminded her hotly.

"Can I help what he says?" Frustration rising, she searched Noah's face, finding only anger. "Apparently I can't help what you *think* either! I'd wanted to see you—to explain—before I left, but I can see you're not ready to listen," she said, feeling irritable and disappointed.

Noah rose from her desk chair, his expression pained. "So, you are going then?"

"No! I mean—I'm going out to dinner! That's all! I have to, Noah. I should have talked to Gary before now."

"Why? To break off your engagement?"

"We are not, and never have been, engaged. I came to Florida to get away from him! He'd asked me to marry him, but I wasn't sure. I didn't know what I wanted! And when I realized he had no place in my life, I should have told him immediately. But I put it off. I—I wanted first to be sure of us."

Her voice hung low in the air, cutting through layers of emotions as she came toward him slowly, cautiously, and slipped her arms around his neck. Noah stood unmoving as she told him, "There's no one else—only you."

Involuntarily, he seized her, pressing himself against her in a furious embrace. His lips came down on hers hard. Then abruptly he set her away from him, so that she had to catch herself from falling.

"Why do I have the feeling you don't believe me?" she asked, shaken.

"Oh, I believe you all right," he said, and she winced under the heavy bite of sarcasm. "What I want to know is—why? Why are you no longer interested in this Woodward fellow? He's handsome enough. And from the position he holds, I'll assume he's reasonably intelligent. So, what is it? Money? The Seaton estate?"

"What?" She sat on the desk as her knees gave way. "That was completely uncalled for. Oh, go away, Noah! Just go!"

"Candle, I—"

Her hand shooed him away. "I won't defend myself to you, so there's nothing more to say. Please leave. I have to get dressed."

She hoped he hadn't heard the catch in her voice as she stilled herself, waiting for the door to close. A good cry might ease the ache inside, but there was no time for that. She'd kept Gary waiting long enough already. Too long, she thought regretfully, dreading the night ahead.

For a moment she sat holding back the sting of tears, wishing futilely that she could erase the harsh words and misunderstandings that had arisen between her and Noah. But she couldn't change his accusations or his attitudes, and even her poor handling of the situation with Gary had not deserved that. *Lord, help him to know the truth,* she prayed.

Gary had to know the truth too, she realized as she tugged off her beige, twill pantsuit. But getting him to accept it wouldn't be easy. He'd scarcely reacted when she'd told him she wouldn't marry him, but she knew him well enough to suspect that this wasn't the end of it. Gary Woodward would have plenty to say!

If only she could make him see that they weren't right for each other. . . . If only he'd be *glad* to let her go . . . But such thoughts were futile.

172

He's waiting, she reminded herself as she headed toward the closet. Waiting for dinner with his attractive fiancée. He couldn't help but be disappointed, yet maybe she could lessen that for him. Pulling out Marcy's tannish-gold dress, Candle slipped it on.

Wearing the unflattering dress and the last traces of makeup she'd had on all day, she descended the stairs, with the carbon copy of Noah's outline tucked under her arm. Her heels clicked, and hearing, Gary came into the foyer.

"You took long enough. I thought you were making yourself beautiful, but . . ." He hesitated then added ungraciously. "You look lousy, Candle! Florida doesn't agree with you!"

"Maybe you're seeing me in a clearer light," she said as he opened the door. "Absence does not make the heart grow fonder."

He grumbled as they stepped outside. Rain-washed, the evening sky faintly twinkled with early starlight, and the air, salt-seasoned, felt cool and fresh. Candle inhaled deeply, refreshing herself on this stale occasion, and thus fortified, she got into the limo Gary had rented.

They had little to say to each other as Candle directed him to the steak and seafood restaurant she'd visited once before, alone, and she wished she were alone right now. She supposed she would be soon enough, and so she forced herself to make small talk, asking Gary about his trip and how he'd been.

"Missing you," he said, but she doubted that would last too long.

Inside the candlelit dining area, a dimpled waitress, young and shapely, seated them next to the window before handing them menus and reciting the evening specials. Taken with her lilting accent, Gary flirted with the young woman while

Candle recalled the many times his attention had been drawn to a pretty face, a buxom figure, a nicely curved pair of legs. She felt no jealousy, only relief that their relationship would soon be over.

"Gary, I'm sorry," she said as she placed a hand on his arm, "but I can't marry you. You know that, don't you?"

To her surprise, he covered her hand with his own, stroking it lightly. "I thought you'd say that, and I could persuade you otherwise," he challenged, "but let's not spoil our dinner, arguing. Tell me about that book you're working on."

If his gesture had astonished her, his words did even more. Perhaps she'd misjudged his sensitivity or caring.

"There's so much to tell, I hardly know where to begin. Here, I brought this along," she said, handing him the manila folder she'd had tucked away on her lap. "The idea is good, and there is a market—I'm sure of it."

"So you said in your letter."

With a slow wink at the waitress who'd returned with a water pitcher, Gary paused, and when the goblets were filled, he went on, "Candle, you know we don't do many religious books."

She nodded. "But this one is different."

"How?"

If he hadn't expressed his interest, she would've thought it completely lacking even though he'd asked. And so, over their salads, she did her best to charge him with some of her enthusiasm for the book, still unwritten. Briefly she recapped the theme, the highlights, then gave a couple of anecdotes to illustrate. But, for the most part, she dwelled on the advantages to Woodward Publishing—the marketing potential, the wide audience appeal, the generous profits if properly advertised, and even the prestige of publishing such a book. However, by the time their steaks had arrived, pink and tender, Gary looked increasingly bored.

Candle sighed. She'd expected him to look at the outline and listen to her ideas, and he had. But if she'd anticipated a positive response, she'd only set herself up for disappointment. *False expectations,* she mused. How easily they crept in.

"Thanks for hearing me out," she told him now.

"That's it?" he asked with such relief, she smiled.

"Yes, I'm finished." She pushed aside her half-eaten steak too.

"Then it's my turn." For once Gary waved the waitress away with scarcely a glance. "I admit I don't share your passion for this project, Candle, but for you—ah, that's another matter!" He gave her a handsome smile. "You realize, don't you, that the book will require a lot of time and publicity effort?"

"Yes," she said slowly, warily.

"And, you are the *only* person who could give it proper attention."

"Go on."

"Come back with me! Then follow through on the book yourself," Gary proposed with more interest than he'd shown all evening. His voice held, in fact, a note of triumph as though he had her exactly where he'd intended.

The night-darkened window mirrored the flickering flame-light and, above it, her face, downcast. From his reflection, she could see Gary still talking, but she scarcely heard him as she buried the spark of hope, heaping ashes on her own foolishness in presenting the book idea to him.

" . . . a vice presidency—immediately, of course, and then when we're married . . . Well, what would you say to being co-publisher of the firm?" Gary went on eagerly.

She barely heard his offer, and so her adamant *no* came unexpectedly to them both. And then, awakened, she told him once again, "I'm not coming back with you. I'm not going to marry you—ever."

He tossed the manila folder at her crossly. "Maybe your next fiancé will publish it!"

"Maybe." Carefully she folded her napkin and set it on the table. "I'm sorry, Gary, that nothing worked out the way either of us wanted." She rose, chin tilted high.

"Don't you walk out on me!" he commanded, and heads snapped in their direction. Abruptly he stood up, almost knocking over his chair.

"Could we talk outside?" she asked in a voice purposefully low. Then grabbing the book proposal, Candle left the restaurant. While Gary paid the bill, she leaned against the rented car, feeling shaken. This was a Gary she had never seen! She'd known he was used to getting his own way, and he wouldn't like taking no for an answer. But by prolonging the situation, she'd only made it worse. If she'd trusted her intuition . . . if she'd had more faith in Noah's book and her ability to help write it . . . if she'd trusted God to direct her to a publisher—and to a genuine love—none of this would have happened. Ashamed, she had to admit to herself she'd tried to use Gary, as surely as he'd tried to use her, by presuming on their relationship. And look what a mess she'd made. Unless the Lord intervened, she'd lost two men—two jobs—in one night.

One of those men was barking at her now to get in the car! Once inside, Gary leaned across the bench seat and took her by the shoulders. "What is it you want, Candle?"

"Nothing," she said, beginning to be afraid of him. "I told you—I don't love you."

"Love!" he spat out the word. "What's that? I know you're attracted to me—"

"That's not enough! I want friendship, caring! I want more."

"I want you." Roughly, he jerked her toward him in the unlit parking lot. "This isn't a game, Candle."

"I never meant for it to be! Gary, let go! You're hurting me!" She threatened to scream, but that only seemed to infuriate him more. And so, deliberately, she went limp.

Eternal seconds hung, suspended, until his outrage subsided. Then he pushed her away, knocking the breath out of her as she slammed against the door. The impact made her queasy, but it helped her find the handle, lodged against her spine, as Gary began abusing her with words. Her mind censored the low blows to her ego, as she fumbled blindly, trying to unlatch the door. Mercifully, it swung open, and she leaped backwards out of the car.

She took off running across the dark pavement, her long legs like a gazelle in flight. Gary would have no trouble catching up with her by car, but, thank God, the only vehicles allowed on the sand at night belonged to the police or beach patrol. She didn't think he'd risk their wrath, nor did she expect him to come chasing after her by foot. But, just in case, she didn't want to face his ugly mood again.

When she'd placed the short distance of pavement between them, she slowed, hopping on one foot in the dry sand drifts as she removed her high-heeled sandals. Then she raced along the spongy, wet shoreline until her breath ran out.

Looking over her shoulder, she jogged along, panting, until she'd convinced herself that the pursuing shadows were not Gary. Her back hurt from his shove against the car door, and her muscles cramped from the strain of running so far, so tense. She guessed she'd gone two miles—maybe three— with still another to go when she finally slowed to a brisk walk. Immediately fear overtook her, and she began to run again until she had no choice but to stop. Heaving, she threw up on the sand.

It was so awful! Not just Gary's behavior, but her own. Not just Gary's anger, but Noah's accusation. Not just this moment, but the misery to come.

Feeling wretched, she dragged herself along the beach, too upset to pray, too tired to care about the odd looks thrown to her by casual, night-time strollers. Someone asked if she needed help, but she shook her head and kept on going, crying softly. Her nose ran until she'd soaked down both sleeves on Marcy's dress, but it didn't matter. They were torn anyway.

Calmly, steadily, the ocean waves rocked back and forth against the shore, lulling and enabling her to gain her bearings. She'd come farther than she'd thought! With relief overwhelming, she saw the familiar pink stuccoed walls and tiled roof gleaming in the moonlight—welcoming, promising security. Upstairs, Noah must have opened a window in his study because she could hear Chopin as she neared, the last notes lingering in the darkness. Then the second theme of Rachmaninoff's Concerto drifted above the ocean swells, and she raced to the sea wall with a new burst of energy.

She couldn't go in! She couldn't risk facing Noah and a thousand explanations—not like this! With the music playing and so many lights on in the house, he had to be up—perhaps even waiting—but she couldn't see him now. She just couldn't.

Huddled in the darkness, she began to shiver uncontrollably—a combination of shocked nerves, sapped strength, and the cool night breeze. Vigorously, she rubbed her shoulders, trying to get warm, and when that failed, she remembered a stack of clean, thick beach towels Noah kept in the pool house. If she could get inside without being seen, she'd have a warm place to rest and to wait for someone to turn out those glaring, revealing lights.

He was mad at her, she remembered, shivering. He'd accused her of—of . . . Oh, she couldn't think. She was too cold, too tired. *Noah is mad. Gary is mad. The man in the pulpit, the man in the moon . . .*

178

Crouched low, she crept along the sea wall and around the gate into the pool house. Stumbling in the darkness, she found the towels and wrapped herself tightly in a terry cloth cocoon, then, shaking, she scooted into the far corner of the oak-slat bench used for changing.

Rebecca Townsend. Rebecca Townsend. What was it about her that she had to remember? Something about Noah. Something about his church. Something about her belonging. No, that wasn't right—it couldn't be. She didn't belong to Noah's church, did she? But she had to, she had to, she had to, or she couldn't belong to Noah.

Throwing off the blanket of towels, she struggled to think, to concentrate, and when she did, a coherent wave of cold irony hit her. She'd refused to marry Gary Woodward because she didn't love him. And she couldn't marry Noah because she did.

chapter
16

OUTSIDE LIGHTS FLASHED ON, flooding beneath the pool house door, but Candle didn't notice. Nor did she care when Noah came in, finding her with her chin propped against her knees. Startled, he called her name, and when she didn't answer, didn't stir, he moved toward her cautiously, as one would approach a cornered creature.

"Are you hurt?" he asked gently, and when she didn't respond, he asked again and then again until, wearily, she shook her head.

She felt like she were at the end of a long, long tunnel with Noah's voice, echoing, so far away. For a moment, she thought she was asleep, nestling against her pillow instead of him, but pillows don't have arms for holding, and they can't check for broken bones, blood, or bruises—which was apparently what Noah was trying to do. Without enough energy to succeed, she tried to pull away.

"Be still," he said. "Are you sure you're not hurt?"

"I'm fine, Noah," she said in a voice that sounded drained, drugged, even to her. "Just tired . . . I ran . . ." She waited for another breath to come and carry off the words. "Three miles—four . . ."

Candle was vaguely aware of Noah's arm muscles tightening across her back, but the hand that pushed her hair from her eyes was ever so gentle. "Why, Candle? Did Gary harm you?"

"I ran," she repeated, and in spurts, she added, "He was angry. I wouldn't go. Poor Gary."

Her eyes hurt and she closed them. Drifting, drifting out to sea, she floated in Noah's arms. "I don't want to," she told a passing seagull.

"What? You don't want to what?"

"Leave Noah."

"Then you don't have to," the gull said, wisely.

"I love him. But—"

"But what?" it asked, brushing her face with its wings.

"I don't know. I don't know!"

"It's okay. Don't cry," the gentle creature said as it carried her away.

She dropped onto a raft with the sun shining first in one eye, then the other. A pair of dolphins stood over her, one holding her wrist and saying, ". . . too low. No injuries, though. Keep her warm."

"Can't you do anything now?" the other said in a voice very much like Noah's, but infinitely sad.

"She's exhausted, and she's sleeping naturally. I can't think of anything better than that."

"Don't go," she called when she heard them leave. Then the sad, sad dolphin was there, holding her close, until the moon somersaulted in the sky.

Someone had poured cement on her eyelids and glued her lashes shut. She tried to rub them, free them, but her arms were leaden beneath the heavy blankets. Grumbling, she stirred.

"Candle, can you hear me?" a voice asked with concern.

"Of course I can, Noah. I'm not deaf."

"Can you open your eyes?"

"Uh-uh. They're stuck."

She heard water running, and then he was back, patting a steamy cloth against her eyes. Even so, she had to raise her eyebrows as far as she could to get her lids opened. When she did, she saw Noah sitting on the edge of her bed, looking even more worried than he'd sounded.

"Is something wrong?" she asked.

"I don't know. I'm waiting to find out."

From the looks of him, he'd been waiting all night, she thought, and then she remembered he had.

"Oh, Noah, I'm really sorry," she said, struggling to free her hand. She wanted to touch his face and ease that line that creased his forehead, but her fingers traced his mouth instead. "I must have given you a scare."

He kissed her fingertips. "Do you remember what happened?"

She groaned. "I'd rather not—I behaved so badly!"

"*You* did! What about that . . . that Woodward person!" He must have terrified you, Candle! You ran several miles down the beach to get away from him. No wonder you were exhausted!"

"It wasn't just him, Noah." Oh, how could she explain? "It was not fitting in. It was Rebecca Townsend. It was not trusting God—or me—or you—or . . . Noah! I lost the outline for your book! I don't have another copy!"

"Relax. It's on your desk. I found it in the pool house. Why were you in there anyway?"

"I was cold! I couldn't come in, not like this. Besides . . ." Her heavy lids slammed shut. ". . . you were mad at me."

The smell of coffee wafted past her nose, and something wet trickled against her cheek. She opened her eyes to find Noah leaning over her, giving her a shake.

182

"Why are you shaking me? Are you still angry?"

"If I were, I wouldn't be shaking you," he said. "I was waking you up. You fell asleep again, and you were crying."

"Oh." She wondered why, and when she remembered, he seemed unbearably close. "The coffee smells good. May I have some?"

Moving away as she'd hoped he would, he poured a cup and handed it to her. "Candle, I'm the one who behaved badly. I wasn't angry at you. I was angry at myself for what I was thinking, what I was feeling. Woodward's arrival caught me off guard."

"I know." She reached out a hand. "I should never have written him about the book. I shouldn't have . . ." She stopped, suddenly awakening to her surroundings. "Noah! Is that Marcy's dress on the chair?"

"It's the one you had on last night."

"How'd it get over there?"

"That's where I put it. Do you want a robe?" Even as he spoke, he went to get it from the hook on the bathroom door.

"I'm not used to being dressed—or undressed," she said, flushing, as she put the robe on over her slip and slapped away his gesture to help. Her embarrassment seemed to amuse him.

"Do you have to sit on the bed?" she asked, irritably.

"No," he said, but he didn't get up. "Candle, did you mean what you said last night?"

"What?" she asked, wearily.

"That you love me?"

"I didn't say that! I mean, I didn't tell *you*." She tried to think. "It was a dream . . . I told a seagull."

"Did you mean it?"

"Would I lie to a seagull?"

She knew he was going to kiss her, and she thought she

really should stop him, but she didn't want to—not when the memory might have to last for a long time. She treasured the butterfly brush against her forehead, her eyelids, her nose, and when his lips settled on hers, she felt an ionic charge like she'd never felt before—from Noah or anyone. All traces of tiredness fell away, and she kissed him back with an intensity, an ardor she didn't know existed. Even his fingertips, combing through her hair, sent waves of electricity through her as he urged her toward him with increasing hunger.

They were lying on her bed! Reluctantly, she twisted away from him as his lips ignited her neck and throat.

"Noah!" She sat up. "We can't . . . !"

"I know." He nuzzled her hair. "Let me hold you a minute. You're trembling."

His breath felt warm against the top of her head as she buried her face in his chest, and his arms felt safe around her, making no demands. She wished she could tell him all that was going on in her head, but she could make no promises until she knew she could meet a deeper need.

When she tugged at his arms, he let her go, and she climbed out of bed with regret. It would be so easy to tumble back into a gratifying moment where she'd felt impassioned and alive and almost his, but almost wasn't good enough—not for Noah, not for her.

In anger, he'd said there was a lot they didn't know about each other, and she wondered if he meant it, wondered more if it were true. As she stepped into the shower, she realized she had an advantage in being in *his* home, meeting *his* grandmother, seeing *his* church—all parts of him he couldn't separate from himself, and she knew he shouldn't have to lose even the smallest pieces of what he was in gaining her. He'd lost too much with Tasmine, and the scars were tender still.

What would she lose, she wondered as she shampooed her

hair. Not her identity—not her personhood. Noah placed no cold compresses on her spirit, her dreams. He brought out the best in her, even when she felt awkward in the first fearful light of discovering. But would she ever discover the joy, the fulfillment, the deep need awakened for him in his church. If not . . . She couldn't bear to think of the loss.

She'd towel-dried her hair and slipped into a comfortable terry jumpsuit before she bothered to look in the mirror. Presumably, her eyes were less puffy and her skin less pale than they'd been earlier, so she couldn't imagine what a mess she'd been last night. No wonder Noah had seemed worried! But fortunately, emotional and physical exhaustion were ailments sleep could cure. Eighteen to twenty hours, she figured, glancing at the clock beside the bathroom sink. Almost dinner time. Having skipped two meals already that day, Candle hoped the last one would be early.

Still, she wanted Noah to take a short walk with her before then to stretch the knotted muscles in her legs. She had to talk to him, and the beach seemed more appropriate than her bedroom had been.

When she entered the sunroom, he was waiting for her on the balcony, and she saw he'd changed into a pair of gray slacks and matching shirt—somber, perhaps, but not as wrinkled as the clothes he'd had on earlier. He didn't hear her bare feet on the carpet, and so she came up behind him, putting her arms around his middle and giving him a squeeze.

"You're feeling better," he said, turning in the circle of her embrace until her hands dropped, abruptly, to her sides.

She'd never seen him in his clerical collar before, and now it seemed a cruel intrusion.

"Oh. Are you going out?"

"For a little while. I won't be long." His hand slid under her chin, tilting her face up toward him. "Look at me,

Candle," he commanded softly. "I'm not a stranger. Can you put your arms around me?" he asked as his went around her.

Clumsily, she did so, and he bent his head to kiss her—lightly at first and then with sparks searing. On tiptoes, she wobbled and pulled away.

"Do you have time for a short walk?" she asked, omitting the talk part.

"If you're up to it."

"I need some fresh air"—which was more true than ever.

Deliberately, she made herself hold his hand as they walked down to the low edge of the sea wall. She wanted to touch him—to test herself, to know if she could accept this part of him—just as she'd wanted him to accept the attractive part of her. He seemed so foreign to her in his clerical dress, which made her sad and yet more empathetic with his response when he'd first seen her in full makeup and flattering clothes. He'd been angry; she felt sad—and both emotions, she realized, resulted from not getting one's own way. *Your way, Lord,* she prayed now as they strolled along the wall.

Noah suggested they sit down, his concern for her still evident, and when they did so, his left side touched her right, generating instant heat. Candle shifted toward him, leaning her head against his shoulder.

They sat quietly a moment, listening to the pulse of the ocean—the steady, timeless drumming that occasionally rose to the sound of thundering applause. "Sometimes I come down just to hear the beating of the waves," Noah said, and she knew what he meant. The muffled sounds, the pulsing rhythms held the comfort, the protectiveness of a womb that gave the feeling of new birth, renewal.

Beneath the low ledge, the wind whistled, and the incoming tide washed seaweed toward their dangling feet. The seaweed looked like the discarded spines and seeds of white concord grapes, and when Candle noticed it, she thought of giants having a banquet feast. She told him, and he laughed, but when he turned to her, his eyes darkened with seriousness and longing.

His delicate kiss took wings as her lips parted, and she tilted back her head, feeling the explosive impact, but this time he didn't have to urge her arms around—they went of their own volition. She clung to him until they both realized she was crying.

"What is it?" he asked with such tenderness, she ached even more.

She sniffed, careful not to drip on his shirt. "I can't stay here, Noah. We're too . . . too *aware* of each other." She groped for the right words. "Rebecca Townsend has set some gossip astir at Trinity, and that's bad enough for you to have to face. I'm confident that God will protect you—vindicate you—as he's promised, and somehow he'll work it all to your good. I trust him. I trust you. But if we stay under the same roof—"

"You're afraid the rumors will be true." He sighed. "I know what you're saying, Candle—that we can count on the Lord's help when we're obedient to his principles. But, you're also saying you're not sure if you can trust me to have enough willpower."

She couldn't deny that, but she added, "Maybe I don't trust me, Noah. Maybe it'd be so tempting to get our lives entwined that we wouldn't stop to choose! Last night when you were angry, you wondered if you really knew me. You certainly don't know my family—my parents—and that's important too. But maybe *I* don't know me, Noah! Oh, I know I love you, but do I fit? And do you love *me?* Your hesitancy to tell me must be for a reason!"

"I didn't want to rush you. I wanted *both* of us to be sure." He sighed again. "I haven't always been so cautious."

"It's okay, Noah. You don't have to explain."

"I told you that my first marriage was a mistake. I know that doesn't excuse me for misjudging you, nor for being so hard on you when I discovered the woman of my dreams was the woman of *everybody's* dreams! I've been through that nightmare before."

"People are different, Noah, but it takes time to know that, time to be sure. You were right not to rush, you or me, but circumstances have made it impossible to be casual, and we're not ready for decisions. Commitments are too important to me, and when I make them, it must be without any reservations. I want no less from you."

"What are you suggesting?" he asked with some of the old caution back in his voice.

"Space. Distance. I can't do that here, working beside you every day. Believe me, I've tried! But," she hurried to assure him, "I *did* commit to helping you with your thesis, and I intend to see that project through. I've been thinking about it, and it's simple, really. You can drop off your notes and tapes with Mrs. Powers as you finish them, and when I'm done, I'll do the same." Even as she said it, it seemed so coolly business-like. Or perhaps the coolness came as Noah pulled away.

"Is that it? Is that all the contact we're to have?" he asked, dismayed. "Won't you at least allow me to see you?"

"I—I don't know." She hated the icy barrier that arose between them, but how could she promise to see him, touch him, be near him again? Unless she could participate fully, belong, in the church, she had too little to offer him that he needed. Seeing him again would only prolong the hurt.

"Can you tell me where you'll be staying?" he asked, rising to his feet.

"I'm not sure," she answered truthfully. With Brad in Marcy's life, her welcome was no longer assured. And then she needed to clear out her desk at Woodward Publishing and decide what to do about her old apartment. "I'll—I'll call you as soon as I can," she promised.

"Look, Candle, I have to go now—I'm late already," Noah said, looking with irritation at his watch. "But, would you think for a while about this? We could talk when I get back."

Wearily, she shook her head. "There's no point."

Impatiently, he brushed off his slacks. "All right. I won't argue with you. Your mind is obviously made up. I'll contact Mrs. Powers in the morning." His response matched the evening chill.

She might never see him again, she realized, as he stood, looking down at her. She might never taste his kiss again! Without meaning to, she reached out her hand, and he took it, pulling her up—pulling her into his arms. Tightly she clutched him, wanting never to let go, and when her lips found his, she kissed him with a breathless fierceness. He tensed and drew back, frowning.

"Was that a good-bye kiss?" he asked, but she couldn't answer.

"Noah!" she called as he started off without another word. "This is best for both of us!"

Abruptly he halted then wheeled around. "Is it?" The ocean waves applauded his sarcasm. "You may know what's best for you, Candle. But don't ever assume you know what's best for me."

chapter
17

NOAH DIDN'T RETURN FOR DINNER, and Candle still hadn't heard him come in when she went to bed. She slept badly, tossing in a sea of doubts, only to awaken to the conviction that she was doing the only thing she could do. No, she didn't know what was best for Noah. Yes, she had to place distance between them for herself. No, she couldn't stay without drowning emotionally. Yes, she wanted to offer him everything or nothing.

Flinging back the covers, she jumped out of bed before dawn, her body aching with tension and tiredness. She stepped into the massaging spray of a warm shower, letting the pulsating water knead her muscles and wash away the headache that had started in the nape of her neck.

Freshly toweled, she stepped into the sitting room, half expecting to find Noah and yet knowing that was absurd. However, reminders of him were scattered everywhere, and she hurried away, squeezing back another rush of tears. According to her calculations, she had cried more in the last forty-eight hours than she had in the last four years!

Slipping on a one-piece jumpsuit, she frowned at the rest of the clothes hanging in the bedroom closet. They'd never fit into her single, small suitcase! Yet the more trips she had to make, up and down the stairs, the more likelihood there was of bumping into Noah. *Oh, Lord, please . . . !*

Flipping her suitcase onto the bed, she snapped it open and tossed in small, loose items, stuffing what she could into the large pockets of her jumpsuit. Undergarments and nighties filled the bottom of the case until she'd gradually emptied the chest of drawers and closet, making reasonably neat piles. She crammed her shoes around the inner borders, then sitting on the bulging lid, she clamped it shut. The rest she'd carry on coat hangers.

Hurrying to the bath, she squeezed her toiletries into the makeup case, tossing out a few unused bottles and vials to make more room. Then she set the jammed-packed luggage beside the sunroom door, feeling overwhelmed by the clutter on her desk.

An extra box would've helped, but having only one, she deposited the files and tapes, unceremoniously, into large manila folders and sturdy brown envelopes until she had a healthy stack held together by double rounds of string. The typewriter would stay since she could borrow Marcy's—or rent one—but the tape recorder-player was essential, and Noah had another for his use. Unplugging it and winding the cord, she looked around the room to see what she'd forgotten. The dolphins. She shook her head, not wanting to take the piece of sculpture Noah had given her, yet not wanting to leave it behind. A gift. An icon. A reminder. She walked away from the sculpted figures.

A shuffle, a click sounded from the hollows of the house, and Candle wondered what time it was—if it were yet light. Surely no one would be up and stirring at this hour! But she was up, wasn't she?

She lingered, waiting. Then cautiously she stepped to the salt-washed panes of the balcony doors and peered out. The sun was starting to come up, capped in threads of carmine, and the tide-swept beach yawned, pink and fresh, along the mouth of the sea. In these precious hours when no cars were allowed on the sand, a single set of footprints tracked toward the water then veered northward.

She wondered how long Noah had been out there, padding along the shoreline in his baggy sweatshirt and cut-off jeans. With his hands shoved into his pockets and his shoulders hunched against the wind, he looked lost, forlorn, and she ached to race down and join him. Suddenly he bent, scooping a shell, and as he straightened, he glanced back at the house. He couldn't help but see the lights in her windows—perhaps even her outline pressed against the balcony doors where she stood, frozen, and for an instant, he hesitated too. Then, hurling the shell into the sea, he continued up the beach without a backward look.

She had to go. It was time to go. But she watched the shadowy fringes of dawn overtake him before she forced herself to gather her belongings.

Oh, Noah! A sob escaped, but at least she had no fear of awakening him now. Heaping her arms to capacity, she banged along the corridor, inclining herself toward haste rather than quiet. If she hurried, she could pack her car and be gone before Noah returned from his stroll.

"Just where do you think you're going?" Mrs. Cousins asked from the bottom of the stairs, and Candle almost dropped her bundle.

"I'm—I'm leaving."

Hands on hips, the housekeeper stood blocking Candle's passage. "Does the reverend know?"

Meekly she nodded.

"Well, there's no call to sneak off before daybreak," Mrs. Cousins scolded. "Have some breakfast first."

"I can't." She shifted a bulging stack that threatened to go flying. "Noah's up—on the beach—and I just can't say goodbye, Mrs. Cousins. Please . . ."

"Hmmph. I s'pose I'd better help you then." Waving aside any protests, she trudged upstairs and returned, arms full.

Fitting all the parts into her small sports car was like working an intricate jigsaw puzzle, and when it was done, Candle rushed back upstairs to double-check the rooms. Her eyes flicked around until she was satisfied she'd left no traces of herself, and then her gaze settled on the sculpture she knew she couldn't leave behind. Memories might be all she'd have, and this one held special treasure.

"That's everything," she told Mrs. Cousins as she tucked her long legs into the driver's space. And with a pat for the dolphins resting in her pocket, she waved goodbye.

Pink arrows targeted the sun as it came up over the ocean swells, but Candle detoured the beach scene as she directed her car toward Marcy's. Thinking it too soon for her friend to be up and about, she debated whether or not to stop somewhere for coffee, then she pulled into a parking lot in full view of the restaurant adjacent.

Inside, she ordered a cream cheese danish to go with her coffee, and not really hungry, she nibbled at it slowly, keeping an eye on her car. She'd sublet her furnished apartment in New York, and now almost everything she owned had just been crammed into the little red vehicle. Not the most secure situation, she thought, but then what was?

On impulse, she bought a morning paper and sat back down in her booth. The classifieds offered a hopeful assortment of rentals as well as several encouraging columns of available positions. If one weren't too choosy, the possibilities were numerous.

But she had a job, for now anyway, so she concentrated on

apartments, circling those that sounded most promising. Even if Marcy still welcomed her company, it might be best to be alone.

Noah was alone. And remembering the forlorn figure, she knew he no longer wanted to be. Was that what he'd meant when he'd told her that she didn't know what was best for him? Well, he was right; she didn't know. She wasn't even sure she knew what was best for herself! But that was what she had to find out—where she best belonged.

It amazed her, an hour or so later, that Marcy wasn't the least surprised to see her. The sun shone fully around the oceanfront of the beach cottage when her friend invited her inside.

"You forget, Candle, this isn't New York." Marcy poured herself a cup of tea then extended the ceramic pot.

Waving a hand, Candle declined. "I've drunk enough coffee to melt a glacier! But thanks." She settled onto the cushiony sofa. "How did you know I'd be back?"

Marcy settled in beside her, sipping her tea. "Rumors." She hesitated until Candle urged her on. "I decided to take your advice about the Seaton advertising account—anticipate their needs and all that," she reminded. "Nothing's definite, but they are considering my suggestions."

"Marcy, I'm so glad!"

"Me too! Anyway, I've made friends with some of the people in the office there. You know how it is—to get to know the business you get involved with those doing the work."

"And?"

"And there was some talk."

"About Noah and me?"

"I'm afraid so. It seems this woman, Rebecca somebody, called up about a bundle of Seaton Industries' stock she's cashing in, and she had a few choice remarks to make about Noah and his, uh, red-headed girlfriend."

Candle sighed. "I can imagine."

"You know her then?"

"Rebecca? Unfortunately, yes. She created a scene—at Noah's house and at Trinity too."

Marcy's hand flicked away the implications. "Don't worry about it, Candle. The talk will die out soon enough."

"I know, and I'm not worried—not about her anyway." She rubbed the tension that persisted in her neck. "Rebecca really didn't have too much to do with my leaving Noah's house."

"Wanta talk about it?"

"Not yet. Did you know that Gary was here?" she asked, changing the subject.

"You're kidding! This town is bigger than I thought—or my grapevine needs watering."

She tried to smile. "He was everything you said—and less, Marcy. I couldn't believe I'd honestly considered marrying him! But it's very definitely over with him—and so is my job at Woodward Publishing. I suppose I'll have to go back to clear out my desk, but I'm dreading it."

"Then don't do it."

"I have to. When I sublet my apartment, I boxed up all of my books and kitchenware and bric-a-brac and stashed them away in the storage room behind my office. Everything I own is there or in my car."

"So? Pay your assistant—your ex-assistant—a fat bonus to ship everything to you," Marcy suggested as she marched toward the front door. "And now that we have that resolved, let's go unpack your car."

It took little time to settle in, and since Marcy had to get to work, Candle did the same. She spent the day editing and typing, allowing Noah ample opportunity to check in with Mrs. Powers before stopping by the agency herself. When she did, a surprise awaited.

"A word processor!" she exclaimed. "And a printer! Are you sure this is for me, Mrs. Powers?"

"When it comes to Rev. Seaton, I wouldn't dare make this kind of mistake," the woman assured her. "The equipment uses the same software you had at Woodward Publishing, Rev. Seaton said to tell you. So if there's any problem you're to let him know immediately."

"Of course," Candle agreed, feeling slightly stunned. She'd been aware of Noah's thoughtfulness, but she'd never dreamed he would provide her with the very equipment she'd used at Woodword. He must have called them to find out.

Mrs. Powers handed her an envelope too, but Candle waited until she and the compact computer were in the car before opening it, but instead of the instructions she'd expected to find, Noah had enclosed several bills of large denominations. A quick tally showed he'd given her double the already generous earnings she'd received working for him, and she didn't know whether or not to be glad. She counted again, hoping she'd made a mistake, but she hadn't. It was enough to tide her over for several weeks. She supposed she should be grateful, but instead she felt as though he were testing her to see what she would do, and she considered returning every cent! She didn't want his money; she wanted him.

He'd attached a note, telling her he would have delivered the computer himself if he'd known where she was staying. Surely he suspected she was at Marcy's, but maybe this was his way of letting her know he wouldn't track her down.

In a note of her own, Candle thanked him for the equipment and the money, which she insisted was more than enough to cover the rest of her salary, and he needn't send any more. As she sealed the message in an envelope provided by Mrs. Powers, it occurred to her that Noah hadn't sent a check because she might not have cashed it, and that thoughtfulness encouraged her warmly. She was no longer in his house, receiving room and board, and so he'd only wanted to provide for her needs.

With the nice endowment tucked away in her newly opened bank account, Candle was able to take Marcy's advice about having her former assistant ship her belongings. When they arrived, she could scarcely move around her bedroom without bumping into something, but she was determined to keep her work area out of Marcy's living space.

The weeks passed favorably for them both, with Marcy and Brad often out to dinner or a play while Candle's fingers flew on the word processor, rapidly nearing the end of the work she'd committed to do. She'd sent out resumés to a few magazines and one book publisher in the area, hoping to line up an interesting job before the one with Noah ended, and so far she'd received two positive responses, requesting an interview.

She'd had no response, however, on the book proposal she'd sent to several publishers simultaneously, but that, too, was in the works, and she felt good about it. What disturbed her was the necessity of working directly again with Noah should anyone offer them a contract, but after a few sleepless nights, she turned the matter over to the Lord.

The quest for a church was in his hands too, and during the month of April she attended each of the places she and Noah had visited together. She felt certain he wouldn't backtrack with so many other denominations he wanted to attend, and yet she continued to fear that she'd bump into him. In his last note, he'd asked if he could see her—if she'd at least call—but it was painful enough to hear his voice on the tapes, and the thought of talking to him, seeing him in person, wrenched her heart.

To make amends and to let him know he was often in her thoughts, she wrote him a long letter instead of the usual brief note. It was business-like, however, updating him on the projects they shared, and so she wasn't surprised when he didn't answer. The next time, she sent him a humorous card, to lift her spirits as well as his, and told him she missed him. He wrote back immediately, "You don't have to miss me. I'm here," and she felt worse than lousy.

The best she could promise him was a tolerance for his ministry—or the church—and that seemed a paltry offering. She wanted to give so much more than that, but how could she if she received so little herself? As much as she hated to admit it, the services she'd attended so far had left her in neutral gear, which was certainly more pleasant than the old fears and trembling, but still not satisfactory.

She'd long ago explained the problem to Marcy, and so it irritated her that first Sunday in May when her friend asked her, "Why is this so important?"

"I thought you understood! I can't have a whole relationship with Noah if any part of his life is off limits to me!"

Marcy stirred her tea, then poured milk over her breakfast cereal. "Did you listen to yourself?" she asked casually. "You keep talking about a whole relationship with Noah, but is that really the purpose, Candle? What about a whole relationship with God and his people?"

"Ouch! I have gotten off track, haven't I?" She helped herself to sugared orange slices then spooned up a bowl for Marcy. "So, what do I do? How do I find that sense of belonging you have at St. Michael's?"

"Well, you could do what too many people do—come until you know a service so well, it fits like a comfy old shoe."

"That isn't exactly what I had in mind."

"I didn't think so," Marcy said with a smile. "I know! You can come with me so you'll know someone." Then she threw back her head, laughing. "If you could see your expression!" Then sobering, "Candle, I'm not trying to convert you to my brand of Christianity! That kind of thinking is what's caused bloody wars, witch hunts, and prejudices in every denomination. Talk about a family feud! This one's gone on for centuries!" Marcy stared into her emptied bowl. "Make that two thousand years. When God's people insisted on converting one another, Christ died in the crossfire. I guess it still happens."

Candle frowned. "I agree, Marcy, but I don't see what you're getting at."

She spooned up a second helping of oranges. "I'm trying to help you see what *you* want. The reason you don't want to go to St. Michael's, for instance, is that the worship there doesn't express your personal responses to God."

"So what are you saying? That I must first look for a church whose overall worship parallels mine—fits my personality as Noah would say?"

"That's it! Look for the place you appreciate God most fully as the person he created. If you need to express yourself emotionally in worship, look for a church that does that. If you quiet your spirit by kneeling in prayer, look for a church with kneelers! But," Marcy cautioned, "search from your own needs and deepest desires for worship, not from some preconceptions about what worship should or shouldn't be. And, Candle," she added, "if you do this—if you seek worship of God first—then I just know that the fellowship you need, the sense of belonging will follow."

"Thanks, Marcy!" Candle fairly bounced on her seat. "I've been hung up about relationships with Noah and with church people rather than with God. And, yes, the first priority is to seek a place where I can truly worship him."

She pushed herself away from the table and leaped up, face bright. "Marcy, I know exactly where to go! There's a church I've felt tremendously drawn to mentally, physically, and spiritually, but I let fears and hurt feelings get in the way."

"Where?"

Candle laughed. "The one place where I can be certain I will not run into Rev. Noah Seaton!"

Marcy clapped her hands with delight. "Trinity Church in Lakemont!"

"You got it!"

chapter
18

DURING THE ENDLESS DRIVE TO LAKEMONT, a thousand doubts assailed Candle, and several times she started to turn back. What if Rebecca were there? What if other people guessed who she was? What if Jake were ill, and Noah had to fill his own pulpit? What if he'd abandoned his church-visiting since she was no longer with him?

No, she didn't think he'd do that—at least she hoped not! And for the rest, she'd have to take her chances.

She was almost there before she even thought to pray. *Help me to worship you fully, in body, mind, and spirit, and Lord, if this denomination is truly my home, and not just Noah's, then let me know it clearly.*

Immediately, she felt an inner quiet inside herself, but the outside trembled slightly as she parked her car and entered the quaint building.

If she'd expected nudges, whispers, or turned heads, her fears were soon relieved, and the only eyes that caught hers in recognition belonged to Jake. He smiled, and she reflected back his greeting. Reassured, she calmed outwardly and opened herself to the morning's worship.

Musical notes from Bach sent messages of love from the organ, and when the prelude had ceased, the red-robed choir entered with joyous song. A light fragrance, which Candle couldn't identify, drifted after the procession, and the gentle smell awakened her to praise of cedar, lilac, fresh lemon, lily of the valley, sun-dried sheets, jasmine, and all the aromatic wealth God had created.

The touch of a warm hand, a cool one, a strong one welcomed her when Jake invited everyone to greet each other, uniting in a moment of peace. And in the silence that followed, Candle found the tenderest greeting, the most affectionate, as her eyes caught those of Jesus and the children in a stained-glass reminder of his accepting love.

She listened to the sermon with rapt attention, finding strength in the Corinthians passage Jake read. He was talking about the church as the body of Christ and each Christian's part in it! Meant for her ears, this message was no accident, and she rejoiced with thanks to God.

At the communion table, Candle tasted the bread and wine as she never had before, and afterwards, she realized that every one of her senses had been involved in the morning's worship—receiving then giving, appreciation then praise.

Too soon the service ended, and reluctant to go, Candle remained in the pew. People often came here to pray, Noah had said, so she could see no reason to rush out the door! She did want a private word with Jake, however, and she hoped to find him later in Noah's study. But saturated now with worshipful sensory awareness and filled with the Lord's Spirit, she closed her eyes, shutting out the distractions of people moving about, leaving, while she focused on the Lord's abiding presence.

How real he was! How total, how perfect! But even though she lacked completeness herself, she felt no censure of her imperfections, only regret that she'd missed so much so long.

Father, help me to repent—to turn away from my aloneness and toward your church. Help me not to be discouraged, and . . .

A hand touched her shoulder, and Candle's eyelids fluttered open.

"Jake!"

"I didn't mean to startle you. Am I intruding?" he asked softly.

Candle's slender hand stayed his. "I'm glad you're here. I'd planned to look for you in Noah's study, but this is so much better. Do you have a moment?"

Jake laughed. "I was going to ask you the same question." He settled beside her on the pew cushion with its needlepoint design of Christian symbols. "Noah didn't tell me you'd be here."

"He doesn't know I am," she admitted, "and I'd rather he wouldn't for a while. It might be too confusing."

Candle sensed Jake's ability to accept, to understand, and she poured out the conflicts that had kept her away from the church and that now led her back again, in openness, to search.

"And what did you find today?" Jake gently probed.

"I'm almost afraid to commit it to words!"

He smiled. "Newborn hopes are often fragile."

"I'd risk that, Jake, if I were the only person involved."

"Noah?"

"Am I so transparent?"

Jake gave her a lopsided smile. "Actually, no. Which is why I was glad for an opportunity to talk with you alone." He suddenly looked uncomfortable, a trace of embarrassment rising above the clerical collar. "Forgive me, Candle, but I had the audacity to wonder if Noah might need me to—to protect him!"

The musical scale of Candle's laughter caroled throughout the church. Then quickly she clapped a hand over her mouth.

"Oh, I shouldn't laugh in church."

Jake grinned. "Why not? God has used some pretty funny stuff—trumpets blowing down walls, coins from a fish's mouth to pay the taxes—and now he's used your good humor to get me over an awkward moment. He's shown me you're good for Noah, and that's all I needed to know."

"Oh, Jake, I wish I could be that sure!"

His kind eyes fathomed hers. "Now I really am ashamed. You're afraid of hurting him, aren't you?"

Her nod was barely perceptible.

"Don't be," he said firmly. "Noah is vulnerable—who isn't! But he can come to terms with your decision regarding the church, whatever that may be. It's only when those close to him undermine *his* choice that . . . But there! I've said too much."

"No, you haven't," Candle rushed to assure him. "I needed to hear that. Besides . . ." Now she was the one to feel awkward. "This whole conversation is really premature."

"I don't think so." Jake's smile broadened. "My friendship with Noah gives me an advantage in observation, and I must say, he *is* transparent."

Candle's heartbeat quickened, and on the way home, she sang through the miles with thanksgiving. How much she had to be grateful for!

When she reached the beach cottage, she edged her car into the narrow sandy strip alongside Marcy's, then raced up the deck stairs, humming. She hoped her friend would be home, yet she wasn't surprised to find the cottage empty since Marcy had mentioned an outing after church with Brad. It was a lovely day for one.

For the last few days, a damp wind had blown all but the heartiest joggers off the beach, but now the April sun shone forth, beckoning. Standing, restless, at the eastern window, Candle watched a bright red kayak roll against the waves.

Two children, clad in T-shirts and short pants, knelt in the sand with shovels and a bucket, and another child, a little girl perhaps of ten, yanked at a kite string. When an elderly couple biked into view—were they racing?—Candle couldn't be cooped up any longer.

Humming again, she changed into a long-sleeved aqua jumpsuit, then coated her exposed face, neck, and hands with sunscreen. On the way out the door, she grabbed a pear, and when she'd munched it down to core, she offered it up to a seagull on the palm of her hand. The black-capped bird swooped and circled, curious, but would come no closer than five or six feet.

"I thought you guys weren't picky," she scolded when the gull squeaked at her like an unoiled door. "Okay! Okay! Next time I'll bring potato chips," she promised before it flew away complaining.

Loosened by the wind, her hair billowed behind her like a mast of coppery red sails as she ran up the beach, and she felt she could run forever. But, well out of sight of the cottage, her pace finally slackened, and she spotted a mobile snack stand with relief.

She bought a soft drink for herself then added a small pack of potato chips for the greedy gulls who hovered around her, fussing. The salty treat enticed them beyond their usual limits as she began tossing small pieces. The gulls caught the chips mid-air, and Candle laughed, delighted as the birds closed in around her.

With the bag emptied, she moved away and watched with satisfaction as the birds squawked and fluttered, searching with their beaks.

"You're quite a cleanup crew," she said, then sat down on the dry sand, keeping her distance from the feeding site.

Resting on her elbows as she sipped her cola through a

straw, her thoughts drifted as pleasantly as the fleecy clouds overhead. She marveled that she felt so at home on this stretch of beach but especially in church this morning—Noah's church—and she wondered why she'd ever doubted it'd be otherwise. She'd felt part of his house, his household, hadn't she? And more and more she'd felt part of him.

She couldn't wait to tell him, and suddenly she thought, why wait at all? Earlier she'd resolved to give herself a few more weeks at Trinity to be sure. But how could she be more certain than she was now? She'd asked God to show her clearly, and he had—even Jake had said she wasn't premature. Why wait then to find out if Noah's gladness matched her own?

Joyous, she sprang from the sand, brushing off her backside, then she tossed the empty cup and plastic bag into the first trash barrel she ran by. Her energy amazed her as she sprinted down the spongy beach near the water's edge, and she almost felt she could fly.

When she sighted the cottage, however, her gliding stopped with a thud. It was still early afternoon—Sunday afternoon—and Noah would be having a quiet time in his study. She couldn't intrude. Could she? No, she told herself firmly, her good news, her happy hopes could wait.

The wind played with her hair, tickling her face, as she splashed through the ocean's foam. *Ouch!* Something stung at her feet, but bending down, she spied no creatures threatening. She supposed that the lathery salt had found a scratch of a seashell, but she found none, and as she continued her walk, both feet, pricked and needled, began to throb. She stopped.

"Sunscreen!" she yelled, furious at herself. She'd forgotten to coat her bare feet! Her feet were part of her, attached to the same sensitive skin as the rest of her, but unmindful of the pain they were causing, she used them to stomp back to the house.

"This is so dumb!" she told herself as she marched into her bedroom and rummaged carelessly through the drawers. Where had she put that ointment? With lingerie cascading from the bureau, she tracked into the bathroom and jerked open the medicine cabinet. Nothing there.

Her puffy toes screamed, and she quieted them in a cool soak before she remember her makeup case. Sure enough, the half-flattened tube was there along with a scant few antihistamines. She debated whether or not to take one now then decided it was even dumber not to.

She swallowed then sighed. There was no chance of seeing Noah today—or calling—since the cottage still didn't have a phone. She could wrap her feet in dish towels, she supposed, or pillow cases since shoes were out, but the uncalloused soles and pads of her feet were swollen too. It hurt to walk, much less drive. Why hadn't her feet puffed up before, she wondered, then remembered she'd worn sandals, which had shadowed and shielded out the morning sun.

She flopped onto the sofa and lay there, thinking of Noah until her eyelids fluttered closed. She'd wanted so much to see him, and now she couldn't—a problem she'd caused herself—but maybe the Lord had a reason for this disappointing delay. Maybe Noah wasn't ready. Maybe . . .

Tired out by the antihistamine, she slept until the screen door slammed, and Marcy peered over the sofa, frowning.

"What's the matter with your feet?"

Candle shifted them onto the folded towel she'd used to protect the sofa from dampness then eased herself onto an elbow.

"I didn't use sunscreen," she admitted with a yawn. "I forgot they were part of my body." Sort of a reversal, she realized, of Jake's sermon today when he'd talked about Christians being various parts of Christ's body. She hoped the

Lord wouldn't assign her to the job of being his feet! "Where's Brad?"

"Home." Marcy dropped into a chair and flung her legs over the floral-printed arm. "We're both exhausted. Canoed twenty miles up the St. Johns River and used muscles we didn't know we had."

"You will in the morning," Candle predicted, and Marcy groaned.

They chatted lazily talking about Brad, Noah, and Trinity, and lounging as comfortably as sore spots would allow. When dinner time had long passed, they nibbled on sandwiches and fruit.

"Oh! Guess who I saw at St. Michael's today," Marcy said, biting into a papaya. "No, not Noah. Rebecca Townsend's parents. Brad pointed them out to me, and I realized I'd seen them many times—Rebecca too. I just didn't know who they were."

"But I thought Rebecca was a member of Trinity."

"*She* joined Trinity—not her parents—and before that, she attended several other denominations, each one having an eligible, reasonably attractive pastor."

"But why?"

"Prestige? Power? Who knows? Maybe she's jealous of the time and money her parents spend at St. Michael's. Or maybe ministers make a special catch."

Candle leaned back against the sofa arm and closed her eyes. "That's crazy! But, Marcy!" Her eyes popped open again. "That's exactly what Noah complained about when I first met him—he was tired of being pursued."

Would he think her interest in Trinity was also insincere—manipulative—Candle wondered, feeling glad now that she hadn't told him. And then she wondered if it'd ever mattered. Jake had implied it didn't; he'd said that Noah would come to terms with any decision she made regarding the church, but that she mustn't undermine *his* choice. She wouldn't anyway, of course, and apparently Jake sensed that. She hoped Noah would too. But how well did he know her?

Would he understand her motivations? Would he accept the sincerity of her search? How well did he *want* to know her?

He'd said some things couldn't be rushed, and Candle knew that that was true. It'd taken time for her to value and accept the church—the body of Christ—and now she had to give Noah time to find his place in her life, to make his own discoveries. But, meanwhile, she couldn't help but pray: *Oh, Lord! Oh, Lord, let it be soon!*

chapter
19

BY MID-MAY CANDLE HAD FINISHED typing Noah's thesis and packed up the word processor and printer to return Monday to Mrs. Powers. She could always borrow the equipment again if some publisher gave her the go-ahead for Noah's book, but at the moment, she preferred to free up the space in her bedroom—especially since she wouldn't be staying at Marcy's much longer. A magazine publisher in Jacksonville had offered her an editorial position, and she had to let them know soon. But she procrastinated as long as she could, not wanting to make the move.

Noah had made no moves toward her for the last few weeks, and the one time she'd tried to call him at home, he'd been out of town. She hadn't rung again since he'd said not a word about his regret in missing her call. In fact, she'd heard nothing from him. She thought it odd and wondered if something were wrong, or if he'd merely been busy with the last of the tapes. Now, she'd finished them, and gladly so, because his voice, coming through the tape player, was almost more than she could bear.

His silence, however, proved even more tormenting, and she wondered if Jake had been mistaken about Noah's feelings toward her, feelings she too had misread. Or perhaps their separation had made him see her more clearly and in a negative light as had happened when she was away from Gary. She didn't think so, but then, she didn't know what to think.

It wasn't like Noah to go this long without even a brief note, but if anything had happened to him, she felt sure Mrs. Cousins would have found some way to contact her. Or Jake would have told her on one of the many Sunday mornings she'd now spent at Trinity Church. Eagerly, she'd looked forward to those visits where she'd felt so much more than a visitor—she'd felt at home—but tomorrow would be the last. Noah's thesis was done, and he'd soon be in his pulpit, where he belonged, with Candle losing both him *and* the church home she'd found.

She knew she was feeling sorry for herself, and she hated that, but she couldn't stop the grief, nor could she hide it from Marcy. She could, however, do something about her friend's reluctance to leave her alone for the weekend. Brad had invited her along to his parents' home to go deep sea fishing or whatever she liked, and Marcy had threatened not to go if Candle refused to accompany them.

"Don't lay that guilt trip on me!" Candle had scolded. Then giving them a hug, she'd told them, "I love you both dearly, but frankly I'm relieved you're going off for the weekend! Misery does *not* love company when it's trying to work something out!"

They left then, in a flutter of warm goodbyes, and Candle felt she was back where she'd started—alone and wrapped from head to toe as she trudged down to the beach.

Would she always be alone? Would she always be running from pain as Noah had once observed?

Thundering, the ocean waves echoed her question, and Candle let them go, drifting, drifting, drifting, until the sea sounds seasoned her, the sea salts purified, the rhythmic waves washed her mind and spirit. *I have come to hear the beating of the waves. . . .* Her body relaxed in the warm sun.

She felt like she were floating, resting on something unseen, and the tranquil effect opened her mind to the positive power at work in her life. How anchored she'd been by iron will and tight-lipped determination to make things work for herself, for Noah! And her efforts were of no more value than the sea grapes cast aside by the giants she'd imagined.

I'm no giant, she laughed, *and the whistling wind and applauding waves are not my doing.*

But they were *for* her—for love and renewal, for appreciation of their creator, God.

Oh, Lord, she turned to him now, *help me to accept who I've been, to know who I am, and to have your vision of what you would have me to be in Jesus' name.*

Born of water and spirit, a peace enveloped her, cleansing away the doubts and fears and renewing the certainty she'd had in love—God's and hers. And it was enough. It was more than she'd ever known.

Trinity, she knew, was part of that love, and the next morning found her there, no longer grieving. Again she experienced a fullness of worship so totally encompassing that she didn't notice Noah until he caught up with her in the parking lot.

When she saw him, rushing toward her, calling her name, she wondered how she'd missed him, dressed in his clerical collar. But his attire didn't trouble her anymore. It didn't matter. Nothing mattered except seeing him again, and she couldn't have stopped the joy and love from reflecting in her face if she'd wanted to.

He looked at her, astonished, and then he smiled. "You're

the most beautiful woman I've ever seen," he said, taking both her hands. His stare, his glance melted her, and then his dark eyes soaked her up as though he couldn't get enough of her.

"I've missed you, Noah."

"No more than I've missed you. I didn't want you to go," he reminded her. "From the first time you ever smiled at me, I didn't want to let you go."

"But, Noah, I looked like a cheese puff then!"

"Not to me. You're aptly named, you know. When you smile, there's a glow about you I can't describe. My grandmother and Irene saw it too," he said. "But I didn't mean to make your work more difficult for you."

"Make my work more difficult? That doesn't make any sense."

"Doesn't it? I refused your request for a word processor—which you needed—because it would've sped up your work, and I didn't want you to leave."

"Noah!" She was stunned. That was one reason she hadn't seriously entertained.

"All I could think about was getting to know you better," he explained, "but then you left anyway." If she'd expected him to seem hurt by that, he didn't. He looked mischievous. "So, what would you do if you were in my spot?" he asked, teasing. "How would you get to know someone who refused to see you—refused even to phone?"

"I called you!" she protested. "Once. You were out of town."

"Of course I was. How else could I be with you?"

"Noah, have you had too much sun?"

He laughed. "Too much rain actually. Your parents said that's typical for May."

Candle blinked her eyes, not sure if she'd heard him correctly. "You were visiting my family? And you didn't tell me? *They* didn't tell me!"

"They promised not to—it was our secret—but they shared a few about you. I particularly liked the photo of your mother's bathing you in the kitchen sink," he teased.

"Noah! I didn't get to see any pictures like that at your grandmother's."

"Grandma Seaton sends her love, by the way. I spent last week with her, and she agrees with me—that you should come back."

"Noah, I . . ."

"Come home with me, Candle. We'll work on the book. We'll pick up where we left off."

"I think you're forgetting where we left off!" she reminded him.

"Somewhere about here, I think."

He lifted her off the ground to meet his kiss—tender, hungry, searching—and yet for all of its intensity, its longing, it felt comfortable, and Candle knew—she'd come home.

Breathless, she wiggled from his arms and onto her tiptoes. "Noah! We're in the church parking lot!"

"Oh?" He cocked a smile. "We're still here? I thought we'd been transported into heaven, but I've never seen an angel with such pink cheeks."

Her hands flew to cover the flush. "I'm not embarrassed— I'm mortified! Your reputation! Your church! And, oh, I'd hoped it'd be mine too."

For the first time that day, she caught him frowning as he led her to a wrought iron bench in the cooling shade of a spreading camphor tree. He sat her down beside him, turning to her with an expression so serious, she longed to reach out and brush it away. But he'd taken her hands, clasping them tightly.

"There's something we have to get straight, Candle. I want you. I want the person you are. You don't have to change that—not for me or anyone else."

"But I'm not, Noah—"

"Aren't you? Irene told me she saw you here last week—that's why I came today, to see if you'd be here. And under duress, Jake confessed he'd seen you every Sunday for the last several weeks! It's not necessary."

"But it is," she insisted.

Firmly, he shook his head. "Don't you understand? It doesn't matter to me. I love *you*. Not your choice of churches. I want you to find where you belong. Not come here because of me."

"But I'm not. If you must know, I came here the first time to *avoid* you." She laughed at his expression. "It was the only place I knew you *wouldn't* be. I'd wanted to see the choice you had made, but Marcy made me realize that the most important discovery was to find out where I could worship God *himself* with all of *myself*. I don't think it's any accident though that he brought me to Trinity—or to you. I love this place, and . . . Noah!" She stopped, astounded, as his wondrous words took hold. "You told me you love me!"

"Did you doubt that?"

She nodded, so he told her again.

"I love you, Candle Louise O'Shea," he said softly, holding her face in his hands. "I love you with a love that's as deep and steady and timeless as the ocean."

"Oh, Noah, I love you, too."

"Then I hope those are happy tears," he said, taking a handkerchief out of his pocket and dabbing gently at her eyes. "You will marry me, won't you?"

She nodded, unable to speak.

"Your parents thought you'd say yes, so I've already invited them down for the wedding."

"Noah! Am I the last to know?"

"Almost—but that's only fair," he teased. "Even Jake knew

how much I was in love with you before I knew for sure myself." He reached into his pocket. "I hope Marcy'll be as glad as my grandmother was. Grandma Seaton sent this to you," he said, unfolding his hand.

"Her locket! Oh, Noah! That's the locket her father gave her mother when he asked her to marry him."

"It goes back further than that," Noah reminded her. "But she wants you to have it, and so do I."

He fastened it around her neck, then took her into his arms again, apparently oblivious to the knowing smiles of onlookers on their way to the next service. "I'll be back in the pulpit next week," he said, tipping her face up to his. "Is that too soon to announce our engagement?"

She traced his brow, his cheek, his lips with her fingertip, then kissed him lightly. "I think, my darling reverend, we've already been announced."

RENEWAL

I have come to hear the beating of the waves,
to feel the steady drums and long-forgotten
pulse of womb, unticking, and to hear the wild
white-capped applause and whistling wind—
　ancient sounds.

I have come to smell the spraying salt and see
the careless waves drop spine and seed
of grapes, white concords,
feasted on by noble giants, ignoring gods,
who cast away the pods like weeds
　on ancient seas.

I have come to taste the banquet wine,
a water living, laced with brine and sand,
and licking salt-shrunk lips
ironed thinner by will and the fiery sun's
　ancient shroud.

I have come to hear the reading of the Will
—not of death, but Life, and living, His.
I have come to hear what will be, was, and is.
　With ancient need,
in search of Him, I have come.
I have come to hear the beating of the waves.

MHS

ABOUT THE AUTHOR

When MARY HARWELL SAYLER married in 1962, she and her husband Bob moved across the country numerous times before settling in Florida. Each move brought a new church home—sometimes Methodist, sometimes Presbyterian, sometimes Southern Baptist, and now Episcopal—and meanwhile, their children attended schools sponsored by the Lutheran, Roman Catholic, Church of God, and Episcopal churches. The family also attended Pentecostal, Assembly of God, and Disciples of Christ churches, but instead of being confused, they discovered that true Christians are found in every denomination, as one congregation joins another in individual, unique praise of God.

Besides churchgoing and romance writing, Sayler writes children's novels and poems of worship and joy. A local school board member and an instructor for the international Christian Writer's Fellowship, she is particularly interested in helping other Christian writers improve their craft, so she's developed a series of cassette tapes on various aspects of writing.

A Letter to Our Readers

Dear Reader:

Welcome to Serenade Books—a series designed to bring you beautiful love stories in the world of inspirational romance. They will uplift you, encourage you, and provide hours of wholesome entertainment, so thousands of readers have testified. That we might better contribute to your reading enjoyment, we would appreciate your taking a few minutes to respond to the following questions and return to:

Lois Taylor
Serenade Books
The Zondervan Publishing House
1415 Lake Drive, S.E.
Grand Rapids, Michigan 49506

1. Did you enjoy reading *Candle?*

   ☐ Very much. I would like to see more books by this author!
   ☐ Moderately
   ☐ I would have enjoyed it more if _____

2. Where did you purchase this book? _____

3. What influenced your decision to purchase this book?
   ☐ Cover   ☐ Back cover copy
   ☐ Title   ☐ Friends
   ☐ Publicity   ☐ Other _____

4. Please rate the following elements from 1 (poor) to 10 (superior).

☐ Heroine ☐ Plot
☐ Hero ☐ Inspirational theme
☐ Setting ☐ Secondary characters

5. What are some inspirational themes you would like to see treated in future books?

_____

_____

6. Please indicate your age range:

☐ Under 18 ☐ 25–34 ☐ 46–55
☐ 18–24 ☐ 35–45 ☐ Over 55

Serenade / Saga books are inspirational romances in historical settings, designed to bring you a joyful, heart-lifting reading experience.

Serenade / Saga books available in your local bookstore:

Serenade/Saga books are now being published in a new, longer length:

Serenade / Serenata books are inspirational romances in contemporary settings, designed to bring you a joyful, heart-lifting reading experience.

Serenade / Serenata books available in your local bookstore:

#1 *On Wings of Love,* Elaine L. Schulte
#2 *Love's Sweet Promise,* Susan C. Feldhake
#3 *For Love Alone,* Susan C. Feldhake
#4 *Love's Late Spring,* Lydia Heermann
#5 *In Comes Love,* Mab Graff Hoover
#6 *Fountain of Love,* Velma S. Daniels and
    Peggy E. King
#7 *Morning Song,* Linda Herring
#8 *A Mountain to Stand Strong,* Peggy Darty
#9 *Love's Perfect Image,* Judy Baer
#10 *Smoky Mountain Sunrise,* Yvonne Lehman
#11 *Greengold Autumn,* Donna Fletcher Crow
#12 *Irresistible Love,* Elaine Anne McAvoy
#13 *Eternal Flame,* Lurlene McDaniel
#14 *Windsong,* Linda Herring
#15 *Forever Eden,* Barbara Bennett
#16 *Call of the Dove,* Madge Harrah
#17 *The Desires of Your Heart,* Donna Fletcher Crow
#18 *Tender Adversary,* Judy Baer
#19 *Halfway to Heaven,* Nancy Johanson
#20 *Hold Fast the Dream,* Lurlene McDaniel
#21 *The Disguise of Love,* Mary LaPietra
#22 *Through a Glass Darkly,* Sara Mitchell
#23 *More Than a Summer's Love,* Yvonne Lehman
#24 *Language of the Heart,* Jeanne Anders
#25 *One More River,* Suzanne Pierson Ellison

Date Due

APR 2 4 1988		
AUG 7 19		
AUG 2 8 1988		
OCT 1 6 1988		
NOV 1 3 1988		
AUG 1 3 1995		
8/19/02		